endorsed for
edexcel

D0625738

REVISE EDEXCEL GCSE
Spanish

REVISION GUIDE

Series Consultant: Harry Smith

Authors: Ian Kendrick and Sara McKenna

A note from the publisher

In order to ensure that this resource offers high-quality support for the associated Edexcel qualification, it has been through a review process by the awarding body to confirm that it fully covers the teaching and learning content of the specification or part of a specification at which it is aimed, and demonstrates an appropriate balance between the development of subject skills, knowledge and understanding, in addition to preparation for assessment.

While the publishers have made every attempt to ensure that advice on the qualification and its assessment is accurate, the official specification and associated assessment guidance materials are the only authoritative source of information and should always be referred to for definitive guidance.

Edexcel examiners have not contributed to any sections in this resource relevant to examination papers for which they have responsibility.

No material from an endorsed resource will be used verbatim in any assessment set by Edexcel.

Endorsement of a resource does not mean that the resource is required to achieve this Edexcel qualification, nor does it mean that it is the only suitable material available to support the qualification, and any resource lists produced by the awarding body shall include this and other appropriate resources.

For the full range of Pearson revision titles across GCSE, BTEC and AS Level visit:
www.pearsonschools.co.uk/revise

ALWAYS LEARNING

PEARSON

Contents

Audio files

Audio files for the listening exercises in this book can be found at: www.pearsonschools.co.uk/mflrevisionaudio

A small bit of small print

Edexcel publishes Sample Assessment Material and the Specification on its website. This is the official content and this book should be used in conjunction with it. The questions in *Now try this* have been written to help you practise every topic in the book. Remember: the real exam questions may not look like this.

Target grades

Target grades are quoted in this book for some of the questions. Students targeting this grade should be aiming to get most of the marks available. Students targeting a higher grade should be aiming to get all of the marks available.

1-to-1 page match with the Spanish Revision Workbook ISBN 9781446903513

Birthdays

You need to recognise dates in reading and listening questions.

Los cumpleaños

enero   febrero   marzo

abril   mayo   junio

julio   agosto   septiembre

octubre   noviembre   diciembre

Dates

Grammar page 103

Dates in Spanish are easy. You just use regular numbers. Don't forget de!

- 5 de marzo de 2014   5 March 2014
- 21 de diciembre de 2013   21 December 2013

The only exception is the first of the month:

el primero (or el uno) de abril   1 April

Note also:

> You don't use a capital letter for months.

el día anterior   the previous day
el día después   the day after

Mi cumpleaños es el trece de diciembre.   My birthday is on 13 December.

Nací / Nació el 8 de abril.   I / She was born on 8 April.

Worked example   LISTENING 1   target D

LISTENING 21   **Audio files**
Audio files can be found at:
www.pearsonschools.co.uk/mflrevisionaudio

Listen and answer the question.

Who was born on 1st July? Francisco's father

- Me llamo Francisco. Mi padre nació el uno de julio y es gracioso porque mi cumpleaños es el día después.

Listening for numbers

- Make sure you know the numbers 1 to 31 for dates.
- Listen carefully to distinguish between certain numbers, e.g. cinco / quince (5/15), seis / siete (6/7).
- Listen out for mil to help you identify dates, e.g. 2013 = dos mil trece and mil = 1,000. So:
  1986 = mil novecientos ochenta y seis.

 Now try this   LISTENING 2   target D

Listen to the whole recording and answer the questions.

1 When is Francisco's birthday?
2 When is his mother's birthday?
3 In what year were his parents born?

Physical description

Describe yourself and your friends using this vocabulary. Remember to make adjectives agree!

La apariencia física

Tiene el pelo ...   He / She has ... hair

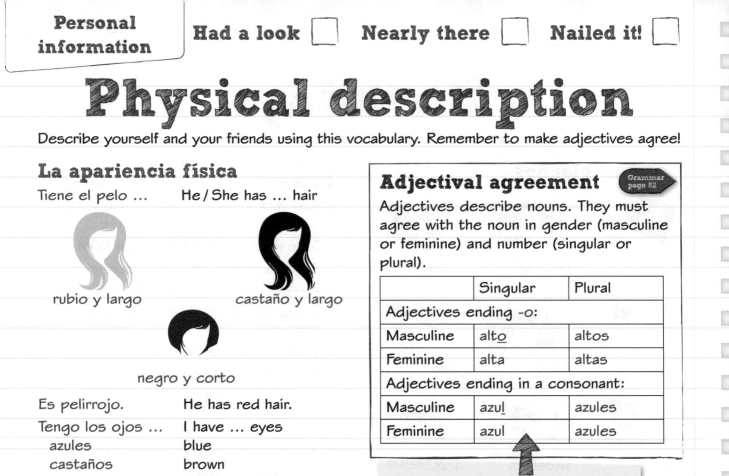

rubio y largo   castaño y largo

negro y corto

Es pelirrojo.	He has red hair.
Tengo los ojos ...	I have ... eyes
azules	blue
castaños	brown
verdes	green
Lleva gafas.	He / She wears glasses.
Lleva un pendiente.	He / She wears an earring.
Soy alto / bajo.	I'm tall / short.
Es gorda / delgada.	She is fat / slim.
Es guapo / feo.	He is good-looking / ugly.

Adjectival agreement

Grammar page 82

Adjectives describe nouns. They must agree with the noun in gender (masculine or feminine) and number (singular or plural).

	Singular	Plural
Adjectives ending -o:		
Masculine	alt<u>o</u>	altos
Feminine	alta	altas
Adjectives ending in a consonant:		
Masculine	azu<u>l</u>	azules
Feminine	azul	azules

Remember: when you're describing hair and eyes, the adjectives need to agree with **pelo** and **ojos**, not with the gender of the person being described.

Worked example

🎧 LISTENING 3   target D

Listen and cross the correct answer.

Manu's father has:

black hair ☐
long hair ☐
curly hair ☒

– Soy Manu y voy a hablar de mi familia. Mi padre tiene el pelo rizado.

Listening strategies

Read the question FIRST so that you know what to listen out for. You might not know the word rizado, but you can work out it's the answer by ruling out 'black' (negro) and 'long' (largo).

Make sure you learn the Spanish words for family members so you know who is being described.

Now try this

🎧 LISTENING 4   target D

Listen to the whole recording and put a cross in the correct boxes.

(a) Manu's mother has blond hair ☐   red hair ☐   black hair ☐.

(b) His father is slim ☐   fat ☐   tall ☐.

(c) Manu's eyes are brown ☐   blue ☐   green ☐.

Character description

This page will help you describe someone'e personality. Remember to use the verb ser for this.

La personalidad

activo	active
alegre	happy
simpático	friendly
generoso	generous
gracioso	funny
responsable	responsible
amable	kind
comprensivo	understanding
hablador	chatty
inteligente	intelligent

Es generosa.

agresivo	aggressive
perezoso	lazy
sensible	sensitive
tonto	stupid
egoísta	selfish
nervioso	nervous
antipático	unfriendly
travieso	naughty
tímido	shy

Es travieso.

Using ser (to be) to describe personality

Grammar page 89

	ser – to be (personality)
I am	soy
you are	eres
he / she / it is	es
we are	somos
you are	sois
they are	son

Soy amable.   I am kind.

Aiming higher

Use a wider range of vocabulary to aim for a higher level. Try to work in words like these:

atrevido	daring
celoso	jealous
mal educado	rude
orgulloso	proud
mentiroso	a liar
avaricioso	greedy
cortés	polite

Worked example SPEAKING

¿Cómo es tu amigo?

AIMING HIGHER Mi amigo se llama Roberto y es muy guapo. Antes era nervioso y un poco antipático, pero ahora es amable y siempre es simpático. Nunca es agresivo o mal educado. Es bastante cortés también. Es un buen amigo.

CONTROLLED ASSESSMENT

In the past, students have often done well in the first few minutes of a presentation, but then struggled when it came to **responding** to questions. Make sure you practise for **both** parts of the task.

Now try this SPEAKING

Answer this question in about six sentences.

• ¿Cómo es tu amigo?

• Make your answer more **interesting** by using qualifiers, e.g. **muy** (very) **a veces** (sometimes) **nunca** (never).
• Work in the **imperfect** to show off your knowledge of different tenses.

Countries and nationalities

If you are writing about a female, remember to use the feminine form for nationalities.

Países y nacionalidades

Soy de / Vivo en		I'm from / I live in
		Nationalities
España		español
Inglaterra		inglés
Escocia		escocés
Gales		galés
Irlanda		irlandés
Grecia		griego
Francia		francés
Alemania		alemán
Suiza		suizo
Estados Unidos		estadounidense

In Spanish, nationalities **don't** have a capital letter.

Talking about nationalities

Like other adjectives, adjectives of nationality agree.

	Singular	Plural
Nationalities ending -o:		
Masculine	suiz<u>o</u>	suizos
Feminine	suiza	suizas
Nationalities ending in a consonant:		
Masculine	inglé<u>s</u>	ingleses
Feminine	inglesa	inglesas

When you talk about people from a country, you always use the definite article.

Me gustan los españoles.
I like Spanish people.

Nationalities with an accent on the ending lose it in feminine and plural forms, e.g. escocés escocesa

Worked example

WRITING

AIMING HIGHER

Write about where you were born.

Nací en Irlanda, aunque vivo en Inglaterra porque mis padres trabajan aquí. Sin embargo, mi madre es estadounidense y nació en Nueva York, así que soy mitad irlandés, mitad estadounidense. Me gustan los ingleses. En el futuro viviré en Londres.

Aiming higher

- The best answers will use THREE TENSES (present, preterite and future), demonstrating knowledge and application of language.
- Using CONNECTIVES makes your writing coherent and more interesting.

Now try this

WRITING

Write about 60 words on where you were born.
- Say where you were born.
- Say where you live now.
- Say what nationality you and your parents are.

- Use the text above as a guide.
- Include **connectives** and a **range** of tenses.

Brothers and sisters

This page will provide you with lots of things to say about your brothers and sisters.

Mis hermanos

Mi hermano está casado.
My brother is married.

Me llevo bien con mi hermana.
I get on well with my sister.

Me llevo mal con mi hermanastro.
I don't get on well with my stepbrother.

Me parezco a mi hermana menor/mayor.
I look like my younger / older sister.

Tenemos una relación problemática.
We have a problematic relationship.

Nos gustan los mismos pasatiempos.
We like the same hobbies.

Tenemos una relación de amor y odio.
We have a love/hate relationship.

Tenemos el mismo sentido del humor.
We have the same sense of humour.

Le quiero mucho.   I love her / him a lot.

Discutimos mucho.   We argue a lot.

Reflexive verbs

Grammar page 88

Verbs which talk about relationships are very often reflexive verbs.

Se parece a mi madre.
He looks like my mother.

Me parezco a mi hermana.
I look like my sister.

Nos llevamos bien.
We get on well.

Using reflexive verbs will show you can use a higher level of Spanish.

Worked example

SPEAKING

¿Te llevas bien con tu hermano?

   Me llevo bien con mi hermano y le quiero mucho. Es muy gracioso.

AIMING HIGHER

   Cuando era pequeño, mi hermano y yo, nos llevábamos mal y siempre discutíamos, pero ahora me llevo mejor con él, ya que tenemos los mismos intereses. Nos gusta la música pop y a menudo vamos ver conciertos. La semana próxima iremos ver un nuevo grupo de mi ciudad.

CONTROLLED ASSESSMENT

Not making any mistakes isn't enough for a good answer. You need to use more complex language and your pronunciation and intonation must be generally good to aim for a higher grade.

This version makes good use of a **reflexive verb** (me llevo bien) and an **opinion** (es muy gracioso).

This version introduces a **second tense** nos llevábamos (the imperfect) to describe what the relationship used to be like. The student has also introduced a **future verb** (iremos), showing good grammatical knowledge.

Now try this

SPEAKING

Look at the picture. Answer the question.
- ¿Te llevas bien con tu hermano/a?

Get a copy of the **mark scheme** for speaking. Mark your own work. Look at marks for:
- content
- communication
- knowledge of language.

Family

If you want to talk about your family, it will be helpful if you can use possessive adjectives.

La familia

padre abuelo madre abuela

hijo hija

mi madrastra	my stepmother
mi padrastro	my stepfather
mi tío/a	my uncle/aunt
mis primos	my cousins
su marido	her husband
su mujer/su esposa	his wife
Están ...	They're ...
prometidos	married
casados	engaged
separados	separated
divorciados.	divorced.

Possessive adjectives

Grammar page 83

Possessive adjectives agree with the noun they describe, not the person who 'possesses'.

	m.sing.	f.sing	m.pl.	f.pl.
my	mi	mi	mis	mis
your (sing.)	tu	tu	tus	tus
his/her/its	su	su	sus	sus
our	nuestro	nuestra	nuestros	nuestras
your (plural)	vuestro	vuestra	vuestros	vuestras
their	su	su	sus	sus

Examples:

mis padres	my parents
sus parientes	his/her/their relatives
nuestra prima	our cousin

Worked example

SPEAKING

¿Quién está en la foto? Háblame un poco de tu familia.

Mi padre está en la foto con mi madrastra. Mis padres se divorciaron el año pasado. Está también mi hermano con su novia.

Accurate use of **two tenses** shows a good range of structures.

AIMING HIGHER Mi padre está en la foto con mi madre. Mis padres han dicho que van a separarse pronto. Mi hermano menor está también con su novia y se casarán el año que viene. Iré a la boda y seré la dama de honor.

The perfect tense **han dicho** (they have said) adds **grammatical variety**. Two ways of talking about the future (ir a + infinitive and future tense) and high-level vocabulary in **dama de honor** (bridesmaid) make the answer even more impressive.

Now try this

SPEAKING

Find a picture of your family. Answer the question below. Talk for about one minute.

• ¿Quién está en la foto?

Add details about your family from other topics, e.g. you could show off your knowledge of hobbies.

Friends

You can use this page to prepare your thoughts about friends and friendship.

Los amigos

Un buen amigo debe ...	A good friend should ...
saber escuchar	know how to listen
ayudarte con tus problemas	help you with your problems
decir la verdad	tell you the truth
estar siempre a tu lado	always be by your side
recordar tu cumpleaños	remember your birthday
ser como un hermano	be like a brother
aceptarte como eres.	accept you as you are.

Creo que los amigos son importantes.
I think friends are important.

Es importante que los amigos se lleven bien.
It's important that friends get on well.

Los amigos están ahí para apoyarte.
Friends are there to support you.

La amistad es más importante que el amor.
Friendship is more important than love.

The verbs deber and saber

deber – should	saber – to know (information)
debo	sé
debes	sabes
debe	sabe
debemos	sabemos
debéis	sabéis
deben	saben

Un buen amigo debe ser leal.
A good friend should be loyal.

Un buen amigo sabe guardar tus secretos.
A good friend knows how to keep your secrets.

Worked example

¿Quién es un buen amigo?

> En mi opinión, un buen amigo debe estar siempre a tu lado, y sabe guardar tus secretos. Debe aceptarte como eres. Creo que los amigos son importantes.

Opinion words (**en mi opinión, creo que**) allow you to access the higher grade band marks for communication and content.

AIMING HIGHER

> En mi opinión, los amigos están ahí para apoyarte, no siempre están a tu lado pero pueden guardar tus secretos. Deben aceptarte como eres. Creo que los amigos son tan importantes como la familia. Es esencial que los amigos se lleven bien. A mi parecer, la amistad es más importante que el amor.

Comparatives (**es más importante que**) show a confident use of more complex structures. Subjunctive clauses (**se lleven bien** after **Es esencial que ...**) show more complex language handled confidently.

Now try this

Answer the question in 30–40 seconds.
• ¿Quién es un buen amigo?

Include **connectives** to make your work more coherent and fluent.

Hobbies

Prepare to talk and write about hobbies using this page. Research any hobbies not covered here.

Los pasatiempos

Toco la guitarra.	I play the guitar.
Bailo.	I dance.
Leo.	I read.
Cocino.	I cook.
Dibujo.	I draw.
Pinto.	I paint.
Voy al cine.	I go to the cinema.
Juego al ajedrez.	I play chess.
Juego con videojuegos.	I play video games.
Salgo con amigos.	I go out with friends.
Veo deportes en la televisión.	I watch sport on TV.
Voy de pesca.	I go fishing.

Escucha música. She listens to music.

Present tense (regular verbs)

Grammar page 87

To form the present tense of regular verbs, replace the infinitive ending as follows:

	hablar – to speak	comer – to eat	vivir – to live
I	hablo	como	vivo
you	hablas	comes	vives
he/she/it	habla	come	vive
we	hablamos	comemos	vivimos
you	habláis	coméis	vivís
they	hablan	comen	viven

- tocar, bailar, cocinar, dibujar and pintar are all regular –ar verbs and leer is a regular –er verb.
- juego, salgo, voy are all verbs which are **irregular** in the present tense. Look at pages 87–88 for more information.

Worked example

LISTENING 5   target F

Listen and answer the question.

What does Fernando like doing? C

A Reading
B Playing tennis
C Playing football
D Listening to music
E Going swimming
F Going shopping

– Fernando juega al fútbol.

EXAM ALERT!

Some candidates struggled with **lectura** and **natación**. Make sure you've revised basic vocabulary like this.

This was a real exam question that a lot of students struggled with – **be prepared!**

ResultsPlus

Listen out for cognates like música / fútbol / tenis as these will help you work out answers more quickly.

Now try this

LISTENING 6   target F

Listen to the whole recording and write the correct letter from above in each box.

1 What does Sandra like doing? ☐
2 What does Ana like doing? ☐
3 What does Luis like doing? ☐

Sport

When you're talking about sport, remember to use the appropriate verb – jugar, practicar or hacer.

Los deportes

¿Qué deporte practicas?	What sport do you do?

Juego ...   I play ...

al fútbol.

al baloncesto.

al tenis.

Practico ...   I do ...

el ciclismo.

el jogging/footing.

la equitación.

la gimnasia.

Hago ...   I do ...

patinaje.

Using jugar and practicar

You use a different verb with different sports. Here are the three verbs in the different main tenses.

	jugar	practicar	hacer
Present	juego	practico	hago
Preterite	jugué	practiqué	hice
Imperfect	jugaba	practicaba	hacía
Future	jugaré	practicaré	haré

Jugaba al squash, pero ahora no hago deportes. El año que viene haré vela.
I used to play squash but now I don't do any sport. Next year I'll do sailing.

Use phrases like these to aim for a higher level:

He jugado al squash pero no me gustó.
I have played squash but I did not like it.

Si pudiera participaría en los Juegos Olímpicos.
If I could, I'd take part in the Olympics.

Worked example

SPEAKING

¿Qué deporte practicabas en la foto?

Siempre practico la equitación tres veces a la semana. Es interesante. En el futuro participaré en un campeonato.

AIMING HIGHER

Practico la equitación desde hace cinco años. Lo encuentro muy emocionante porque es un deporte rápido. Siempre practico la equitación tres veces a la semana. Es interesante. En el futuro jugaré en un campeonato y será divertido. Me gustaría ganar. Si pudiera, participaría en los Juegos Olímpicos.

Using two tenses accurately (practico, participaré) will improve your content and language.

Justifying your opinion (porque es un deporte rápido) introduces more complex language. The addition of the conditional (me gustaría, participaría) gives you a better chance of a higher grade.

Aiming higher

Include opinion phrases in different tenses.

Era interesante.	It was interesting.
Será divertido.	It will be fun.
Es guay.	It's great.

Now try this

SPEAKING

Find a picture of yourself doing a sport. Talk for 30 seconds in answer to this question.
• ¿Qué deporte practicabas en la foto?

• Make a point of using a range of tenses.
• Justify opinions with appropriate adjectives.

Arranging to go out

If you visit a Spanish-speaking country, or your school has Spanish visitors, you may well need to use some of the vocabulary on this page to invite someone to go out!

Las invitaciones

¿Quieres salir el sábado?	Do you want to go out on Saturday?
¿Estás libre?	Are you free?
Podemos / Me gustaría ir ...	We could / I'd like to go ...
al cine / a la bolera / a la piscina	to the cinema / bowling alley / swimming pool
¿Dónde nos encontramos?	Where shall we meet?
¿Nos encontramos en el café?	Shall we meet in the café?
¿A qué hora?	At what time?
Podemos quedar en la estación.	We can meet at the station.
No puedo, estoy ocupado.	I'm sorry, I'm busy.
No me apetece.	I don't fancy it.
Tengo que ...	I have to ...
hacer los deberes.	do my homework.
salir con mis padres.	go out with my parents.
hacer de canguro.	babysit.

Radical changing verbs
(Grammar page 82)

In radical changing verbs, the vowel in the first syllable changes in the singular and 3rd person plural.

	poder – to be able	querer – to want
I	puedo	quiero
you	puedes	quieres
he/she/it	puede	quiere
we	podemos	queremos
you	podéis	queréis
they	pueden	quieren

poder and querer are followed by the infinitive:

No puedo salir.	I can't go out.
¿Quiere ir al cine el viernes?	Does he want to go to the cinema on Friday?

Worked example
LISTENING 7 · *target D*

Listen and put a cross by the correct ending.

Miguel wants to go to the:

sports centre. ☐
disco. ☐
cinema. ☒

– ¡Hola, Andrea! ¿Quieres salir el sábado? Podemos ir al cine.

Listening strategies

This topic is likely to involve the DAYS of the week and PLACES to go. Make sure you have reviewed key vocabulary like this.

EXAM ALERT!

Some candidates struggled with the time **las ocho y diez**. Times come up in all sorts of contexts – make sure you are confident with them.

This was a real exam question that a lot of students struggled with – **be prepared!**
ResultsPlus

Now try this
LISTENING 8 · *target D*

Remember to read the answer options **before** you listen! Then you'll know what to listen out for.

Listen to the whole recording and put a cross by the correct endings.

1 Miguel is bringing his: friend. ☐   mother. ☐   father. ☐
2 Andrea would prefer to go on: Friday. ☐   Sunday. ☐   Tuesday. ☐
3 She suggests meeting at: 7.50. ☐   8.00. ☐   8.10. ☐

Last weekend

Use the phrases here to write or talk about what you did last weekend.

El fin de semana pasado

Jugué al golf.	I played golf.
Hice mis deberes.	I did my homework.
Navegué por internet.	I surfed the internet.
Fui a una fiesta.	I went to a party.
Leí una revista.	I read a magazine.
Me quedé en casa.	I stayed at home.
Ví la televisión.	I watched TV.
Escuché mi iPod.	I listened to my iPod.
Salí con mis amigos.	I went out with friends.
Compré ropa.	I bought clothes.
ayer	yesterday
el sábado pasado	last Saturday
el domingo pasado	last Sunday
al día siguiente	the day after

Habló con sus amigas.

Preterite tense

Grammar page 91

To form the preterite tense of regular verbs, replace the infinitive ending as follows:

	hablar to speak	comer to eat	vivir to live
I	hablé	comí	viví
you	hablaste	comiste	viviste
he / she / it	habló	comió	vivió
we	hablamos	comimos	vivimos
you	hablasteis	comisteis	vivisteis
they	hablaron	comieron	vivieron

Be careful with accents!
hablo – I speak   BUT
habló – he / she spoke

Worked example

Write about what you did last weekend.

El fin de semana pasado jugué muchos deportes. El sábado por la mañana jugué al baloncesto con mis amigos en el parque y después fui a la piscina. El domingo fue el cumpleaños de mi abuelo así que fuimos a un restaurante.

AIMING HIGHER

Normalmente juego al baloncesto los fines de semana pero el sábado pasado tuve que jugar al golf con mi padre porque fue su cumpleaños. Fue la primera y última vez – es tan aburrido. El domingo no jugué al baloncesto porque jugué al hockey y fue muy divertido. Es más, el fin de semana que viene jugaré al tenis con Ana. Será un partido interesante.

This student has accurately used the **preterite** and has also added in some **connectives** (después) to make the writing flow better.

This student has gone beyond just describing 'last weekend' and has managed to include **future tense** verbs too (**jugaré** and **será**). She has varied her writing by introducing **negative phrases** and added **opinions** which can help aim higher in the knowledge of language section.

Now try this

Write about what you did last weekend in about 200 words.

- Give details of any activities you did.
- Talk about what you usually do at the weekend.
- Outline your plans for next weekend.

Remember to show that you can use **three** tenses!

TV programmes

You need to be able to describe the TYPE of programmes you watch, as well as naming them.

Los programas de televisión

los programas de deporte	sports programmes
el telediario / las noticias	news
los documentales	documentaries
los concursos	gameshows
las series de policías	police series
los dibujos animados	cartoons
las telenovelas	soaps
un programa de tele-realidad	a reality TV programme

Note that you always use the definite article (the) for the items you compare.

Aiming higher

You need to give or understand REASONS for your likes and dislikes. Use comparatives to impress!

The comparative

Grammar page 84

The comparative is used to compare two things. It is formed as follows:

más + adjective + que = more … than
menos + adjective + que = less … than

The adjective agrees with the noun it describes:

Las telenovelas son menos aburridas que los concursos.
Soap operas are less boring than gameshows.

Los dibujos animados son más interesantes que los programas de tele-realidad.
Cartoons are more interesting than reality TV programmes.

Worked example

READING   target **F**

Read the text and answer the question.

TVE1 Esta mañana

07.00	Telediario.
08.00	Supermodelo España. Tele-realidad.
09.00	Corazones. Telenovela.
10.00	Rueda de la fortuna. Un concurso.

What time should you watch if you like the news? 07.00

Reading strategies

- Read the questions first to see which three pieces of vocabulary you are looking for.
- If you know that the word for 'soaps' in question 2 below is telenovelas, do that first. Then rule it out as an option for I.
- Remember: never leave a blank. If you're unsure, have a guess.

Now try this

READING   target **F**

Read the text again and answer the questions.

What time should you watch if you like:

1 game shows?   2 soaps?   3 reality TV?

Cinema

Describing the last film you saw is a good topic for a speaking or writing assessment.

El cine

una comedia	a comedy
una película romántica	a romantic film
una película de dibujos animados	an animated film / cartoon
una película de ciencia ficción	a science-fiction film
una película de aventuras	an adventure film
una película de suspense	a thriller
una película de terror	a horror film
misterioso	mysterious
emocionante	exciting
fascinante	fascinating
raro / extraño	strange
terrorífico	terrifying
sorprendente	surprising
impresionante	impressive
infantíl	childish
gracioso	funny
con subtítulos	with subtitles

The superlative

Grammar page 84

The superlative is used to compare more than two things. It is formed as follows:

el / la / los / las más + adjective = the most ...

el / la / los / las menos + adjective = the least ...

The definite article and the adjective agree with the noun described.

Las películas de terror son las más escalofriantes. Horror films are the creepiest.

Note these irregular forms:
el / la mejor – the best
el / la peor – the worst

Worked example

READING   target B-C

Read the text.

En mi opinión, las películas de suspense son las mejores porque son las más emocionantes. Las películas de terror son las peores porque no son originales. **Alejandro**

Creo que las películas de dibujos animados son las mejores porque son graciosas. Las películas de ciencia ficción son las peores porque son infantiles. **Sonia**

• Knowing the **superlative** (las más) is vital to understanding that Alejandro prefers thrillers. Review grammar as well as vocabulary in preparation for the exam.
• When identifying **reasons**, look out for **porque** as a clue.

Aiming higher

Look at SPANISH WEBSITES about films and TV programmes. Not only will you practise your vocabulary, you'll also develop good reading strategies that will help you in the exam, such as:
• using what you know to rule out some options
• recognising cognates
• using grammar structures to help work out unknown words.

Complete the grid in English.

	Favourite film	Reason
Alejandro	thrillers	
Sonia		

Now try this

READING   target B-C

Read the text again and complete the grid above.

Music

Make sure any discussion of music includes your opinions and some personal recollections.

La música

Toco …	I play …
Estoy aprendiendo a tocar …	I am learning to play …

el piano
the piano

la trompeta
the trumpet

el violín
the violin

la batería
the drums

la flauta
the flute

en la orquesta	in the orchestra
en un grupo de rock	in a rock group
Escucho …	I listen to …
la música rock / pop	rock / pop music
la música clásica / folk	classical / folk music

Using different verbs for 'to play'

Jugar and tocar both mean 'to play'. You use jugar for sports and tocar for musical instruments.

Juego al hockey.	I play hockey.
Juega al fútbol.	He / She plays football.
Toca el ukulele.	He / She plays the ukelele.

Toca la guitarra.

Worked example | READING | target **C**

Read and put a cross in the **four** correct boxes.

Pablo Estoy en la orquesta del instituto con mi hermano, que toca el violín. Me encanta la música y toco muy bien la flauta.

Martín Estoy aprendiendo a tocar la batería ya que la música rock me encanta.

Silvia No toco ningún instrumento porque prefiero ir a conciertos para escuchar música clásica. Me encanta el sonido de la flauta.

1 Pablo's brother plays in the orchestra. ☒
2 Pablo's brother plays the flute. ☐
3 Pablo isn't very musical. ☐
4 Martín is learning to play the drums. ☐
5 Martín loves rock music. ☐
6 Silvia likes singing. ☐
7 Silvia doesn't play an instrument. ☐
8 Silvia plays in concerts. ☐

Here, it's very important that you distinguish between **toca** (she plays) and **toco** (I play).

EXAM ALERT!

Sometimes students get answers wrong because they miss the little words that can completely change the meaning.

Some students get questions wrong because they don't look at verb endings carefully enough.

Missing negatives can also mean getting the wrong answer.

Always be sure to read the text very carefully.

Students have struggled with exam questions similar to this – **be prepared!**

ResultsPlus

Now try this | READING | target **C**

Read the text again and complete the activity by finding the other **three** correct sentences.

Online activities

Remember to include a wide range of online activities when you talk or write about this topic. Don't just talk about using the internet.

Las actividades online

Suelo ...	I usually ...
mandar correos electrónicos	send emails
comprar por Internet	buy on the internet
hacer mis deberes	do my homework
chatear con mis amigos	talk to my friends
utilizar los chats	use chat rooms
navegar por Internet	surf the net
mandar fotos	send photos
subir fotos a Facebook	upload photos to Facebook

Talking about what usually happens

You use the verb soler + the infinitive to talk about what someone USUALLY does.

suelo	I usually ...
sueles	you usually (singular / informal) ...
suele	he/she usually ...
solemos	we usually ...
soléis	you usually (plural / informal) ...
suelen	they usually ...

Suelo descargar música.
I usually download music.

Solía ver vídeos en YouTube.
I used to watch videos on YouTube.

Knowing the **imperfect** form can help you discriminate in listening tests.

Worked example   🎧 9   target B

Listen to Miguel and Luz and put a cross in the **four** correct boxes.

1 Miguel often uses the internet for homework. ☒
2 He used to find his friends boring. ☐
3 He enjoys talking to friends online. ☐
4 He sends photos because it's quicker. ☐
5 Luz used to send e-mails. ☐
6 She used to shop online. ☐
7 She thinks using the internet wastes time. ☐
8 She wants to save her money. ☐

- Suelo hacer los deberes cuando estoy conectado a Internet.

- Recognising **suelo** in the present allows you to understand that he is doing something **currently**.
- Knowing that **solía** is a verb in the imperfect shows that activity is in the **past**.
- Take care not to jump to conclusions. In this context **ahora** means 'now' but refers to his opinion **about** the activity, not the activity itself.

Now try this   🎧 10   target B

Listen to the whole recording and complete the activity by finding the other **three** correct sentences.

Daily routine

To talk or write about daily routines, make sure you are confident with using reflexive verbs and times of the day.

Mi rutina diaria

Me despierto a las siete.	I wake up at seven o'clock.
Me levanto	I get up
Me ducho deprisa.	I shower quickly.
Me lavo los dientes.	I brush my teeth.
Me cepillo el pelo.	I brush my hair.
Me visto y me pongo el uniforme.	I get dressed and put my uniform on.
Desayuno.	I have breakfast.
Salgo de casa.	I leave home.
Voy al instituto en coche.	I go to school by car.
Vuelvo a casa.	I get home.
Ceno.	I eat.
Me acuesto.	I go to bed.
Me duermo.	I go to sleep.
Siempre estoy cansado.	I'm always tired.

Reflexive verbs

Grammar page 88

Remember: reflexive verbs have a PRONOUN before the verb:

Me levanto.   I get up.

Talking about time

Son ...   It's ...
A ...   At ...

Note the exception:
Es la una. A la una.
It's one o'clock. At one o'clock.

las dos	las dos y cinco	las dos y cuarto

las dos y media	las tres menos cuarto	las tres menos diez

Worked example

WRITING

Describe your daily routine.

Normalmente me despierto temprano, a las seis, pero ayer me levanté a las siete porque estaba cansado.

AIMING HIGHER Mis padres se despiertan a las seis. Siempre me ducho, pero mi hermana se baña. Se pasa demasiado tiempo en el cuarto de baño. ¡Ayer se pasó treinta minutos! Ojalá tuviera mi propio cuarto de baño.

Aiming higher

Using a RANGE OF TENSES accurately will improve your 'knowledge of language' level.

To aim even higher:

• include extra information

• introduce a complex structure.

• This version has added **extra information**, with his opinion of his sister's behaviour (**se pasa demasiado tiempo en el cuarto de baño**).

• It also deserves a higher grade as it includes a **complex structure** (ojalá tuviera) to say he wishes he had his own bathroom.

Now try this

WRITING

Describe your daily routine in about 100 words.

• Include times.

• Mention things that interrupt your routine and say why.

• Give your opinion on things that affect your routine.

Breakfast

This page will help you talk about breakfast and how important it is.

El desayuno

un desayuno saludable	a healthy breakfast
desayuno	I eat (for breakfast)
cereales	cereal
una tostada	toast
yogur	yoghurt
fruta	fruit
con mantequilla	with butter
Nunca desayuno.	I never have breakfast.
beicon	bacon
huevos	eggs
salchichas	sausages
bebo	I drink
con leche	with milk

un café   un zumo de naranja   un té

Days of the week

lunes	Monday
martes	Tuesday
miércoles	Wednesday
jueves	Thursday
viernes	Friday
sábado	Saturday
domingo	Sunday

To specify a particular day, use los:

Los sábados por la mañana desayuno beicon y huevos.

On Saturday mornings I have bacon and eggs for breakfast.

por la tarde / noche	in the afternoon / at night
los fines de semana	at weekends
todos los días	every day

Worked example READING target A

Read the text and answer the question in English.

Un buen desayuno

¿Sabías que el desayuno es la comida más importante del día? Algunas personas no le dan importancia a esta comida y se lo saltan todos los días. Un sondeo revela que los jóvenes que desayunan saludablemente (zumo, tostadas, leche o cereales) sacan buenas notas. El secreto de un buen desayuno es un desayuno saludable, equilibrado y sabroso. Además, se debe evitar bebidas estimulantes, como el café o el té.

What do some people do every day?

They skip breakfast.

Reading strategies

- Always read the TITLE carefully to get an idea of what the text is about.
- In higher level texts there may well be words you don't recognise. Use what you DO know to work out what you don't know.

What can you use to work out **saltan**? The phrase **no le dan importancia** is a big clue that it's a **negative** thing. The worst way you could approach the best meal of the day? To skip it, so **saltar** = to skip.

Now try this READING target A

Read the text again and answer the questions in English.

1 What did a survey show about young people who ate a healthy breakfast?
2 What is the secret of a good breakfast? Give **three** details.
3 What is the recommendation on drinking tea or coffee?

Eating at home

This page will give you some useful structures to make talking or writing about what you eat more interesting.

Comer en casa

el almuerzo	lunch
la cena	evening meal
el helado	ice cream
el pescado	fish
las verduras	vegetables
la fruta	fruit
el pollo asado	roast chicken
los perritos calientes	hot dogs
una chuleta	a chop
el arroz	rice
la sopa	soup
dulce / picante / sabroso	sweet / spicy / tasty
tener hambre / sed	to be hungry / thirsty

— ensalada

— patatas fritas

— carne

To say how long you have been doing something

Grammar page 90

Use desde hace + present tense OR llevo + the gerund:

Como alimentos ecológicos desde hace dos años.
I have been eating organic food for two years.

Llevo cinco meses comiendo pescado fresco.
I have been eating fresh fish for five months.

To say you have just done something

Use acabo de + infinitive:

Acabo de dejar de comer carne.
I have just stopped eating meat.

Worked example
READING · target B

Read the text.
Normalmente hago comidas sanas. Salía comer hamburguesas, patatas fritas y perritos calientes pero ya no me gusta el sabor. Además, no como carne desde hace seis años. Cuando sea mayor, voy a cocinar con verduras de la granja que está al lado de mi casa porque no contienen productos químicos. Acabo de comenzar a comer más pescado porque es bueno para la salud.

Put a cross in the box beside the correct ending.
Paco doesn't like:
fast food. ☒
food grown locally. ☐
seafood. ☐

Learning vocabulary

To prepare for your exam, you need to learn lots of vocabulary.

- LOOK at the words and memorise them.
- COVER the words.
- WRITE the words.
- LOOK again.
- SEE how many you got right.

Start by covering the English words. When you're confident, cover the Spanish words and see if you can remember them from the English prompts.

Now try this
READING · target B

Read the text again and Put a cross in the box beside the correct endings.

1 Paco has: never eaten meat. ☐   used to eat meat. ☐   still eats meat. ☐
2 In future he will eat: organic vegetables. ☐   hot dogs. ☐   more fish. ☐
3 He eats fish because: there's a lot of it. ☐   it's healthy. ☐   his house is near the sea. ☐

Keeping fit and healthy

Use this page to prepare yourself to discuss healthy living.

Estar en forma

¿Qué haces para estar en forma?	What do you do to keep fit and healthy?
Es importante ...	It's important ...
hacer deporte / ejercicio	to do sport / exercise
dormir más	to sleep more
beber agua	to drink water
comer fruta y verduras	to eat fruit and vegetables
no fumar nunca cigarrillos	to never smoke cigarettes
evitar la comida basura	to avoid junk food
no tomar nunca drogas	to never take drugs
ser vegetariano	to be a vegetarian
no beber alcohol	to not drink alcohol
no estar estresado	to not be stressed
porque es peligroso	because it is dangerous
porque es asqueroso	because it is disgusting
no es sano	it's unhealthy

Using Ojalá to say 'Let's hope!'

Ojalá is a word which means 'let's hope' or 'if only'.

Ojalá no fumes más.
Let's hope you don't smoke any more.

Ojalá puedas dejar de comer tantos caramelos.
Let's hope you can stop eating so many sweets.

Ojalá pudiera estar más en forma.
If only I could be more fit and healthy.

These are all useful expressions to include if you want to aim for a higher grade.

Worked example  SPEAKING

¿Qué haces para estar en forma?

Siempre duermo mucho y como verduras. Comía comida basura y bebía cerveza. En el futuro, comeré más verduras.

AIMING HIGHER Duermo unas seis horas por la noche y como verduras y frutas. Comía comida basura y bebía alcohol. En el futuro, no beberé tanto. Me gustaría relajarme más y es aconsejable dormir al menos ocho horas, así que seguiré este consejo. Ojalá pudiera estar más en forma.

Using **three** tenses – duermo, comía, comeré (present, imperfect and future) – shows enough variety to improve the language level.

Lengthening the response with further information (about wanting to relax and sleeping at least eight hours) improves the **content** level. The use of more complex and sophisticated **language** (especially with the **Ojalá** phrase about wanting to be fit) also shows the ability to use a range of structures confidently.

Now try this SPEAKING

Answer this question in about six sentences.
- ¿Qué haces para estar en forma?

You could mention:
- what you normally do to keep fit and healthy
- what you used to do
- what you will do
- whether you have any bad habits.

19

Had a look ☐ Nearly there ☐ Nailed it! ☐

Health problems

The language on this page will help you tackle listening or reading tasks on health problems.

Problemas de salud

enganchado / adicto	hooked / addicted
borracho	drunk
un hábito	a habit
la terapia	therapy
respirar	to breathe
morir	to die
inyectar	to inject
adelgazar / engordar	to lose / gain weight
fumar	to smoke
tomar drogas	to take drugs
parar / dejar de fumar	to stop smoking
SIDA	AIDS
dificultades respiratorias	breathing dificulties
cáncer de pulmón	lung cancer
un toxicómano	a drug addict
las drogas	drugs
un sobredosis	an overdose
resistir la tentación	to resist temptation

Using para to extend sentences

Grammar page 100

Using para (in order to) + the infinitive will allow you to extend your sentences and make your work more interesting.

Fumo para desestresarme.
I smoke to de-stress.

He dejado de fumar para respirar mejor.
I have stopped smoking to improve my breathing.

For higher grades, try using these phrases in your controlled assessment:

Beben alcohol para olvidarse de sus problemas.
They drink alcohol to forget their problems.

Para resistir la tentación de fumar, no salgo con amigos que fuman. Nunca lo probaría.
In order to resist the temptation to smoke, I don't go out with friends who smoke. I would never try it.

Worked example

WRITING *target A**

Give your opinion about drugs, smoking and alcohol.

AIMING HIGHER

Para evitar engancharme al tabaco nunca lo pruebo cuando fuman mis amigos. Nunca lo probaría. Y voy a resistir la tentación de beber alcohol. Algunos amigos siempre beben los fines de semana. Han intentado dejarlo pero no pueden. Beben alcohol para olvidarse de sus problemas. Nunca tomaría drogas para divertirme porque es una estupidez.

CONTROLLED ASSESSMENT

This can be a complex topic. Students who include the following will give themselves the best chance of aiming for a higher grade:

- a range of tenses (present, future with **ir a**, perfect); also the conditional
- an impressive range of structures (negatives and direct object pronouns).
- a variety of opinions, with justifications
- a mix of subjects (I, one, they).

Now try this

WRITING

Give your opinion about drugs, smoking and alcohol in about 100 words.

- You could mention why you think people use them.
- Remember to back up your opinions with reasons.

Aim to include:
- **para** to extend sentences
- a range of tenses
- a range of structures.

The body

Use the language here to talk about illnesses and other ailments affecting the body.

El cuerpo

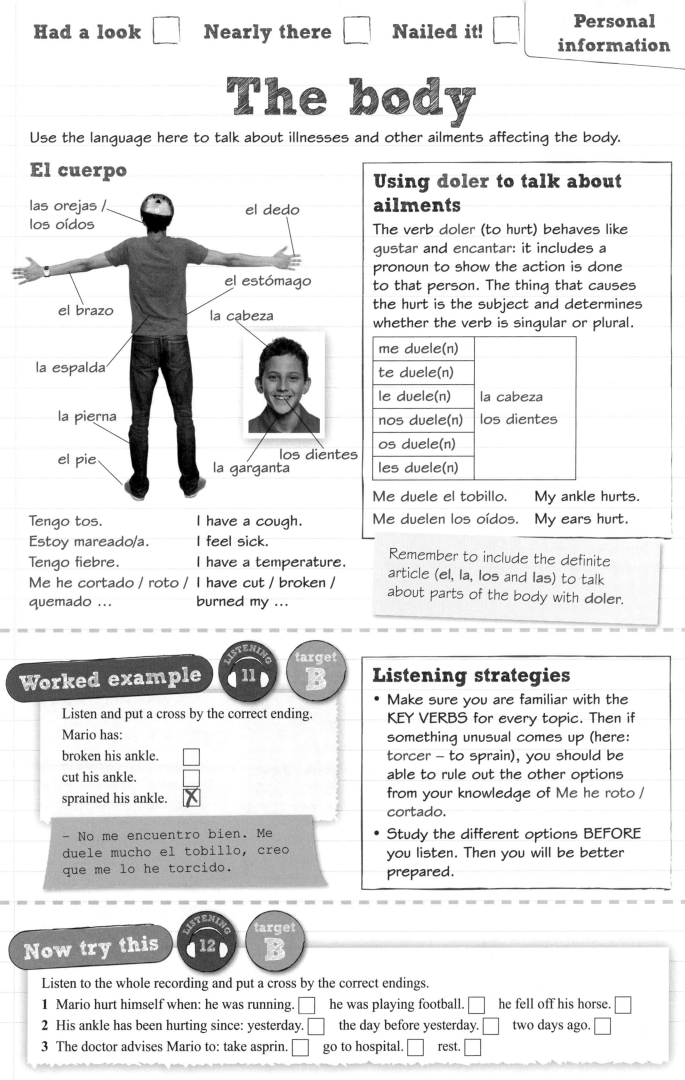

las orejas / los oídos

el dedo

el brazo

el estómago

la espalda

la cabeza

la pierna

el pie

la garganta

los dientes

Tengo tos.	I have a cough.
Estoy mareado/a.	I feel sick.
Tengo fiebre.	I have a temperature.
Me he cortado / roto / quemado …	I have cut / broken / burned my …

Using doler to talk about ailments

The verb doler (to hurt) behaves like gustar and encantar: it includes a pronoun to show the action is done to that person. The thing that causes the hurt is the subject and determines whether the verb is singular or plural.

me duele(n)	
te duele(n)	
le duele(n)	la cabeza
nos duele(n)	los dientes
os duele(n)	
les duele(n)	

| Me duele el tobillo. | My ankle hurts. |
| Me duelen los oídos. | My ears hurt. |

Remember to include the definite article (el, la, los and las) to talk about parts of the body with doler.

Worked example

LISTENING 11 **target B**

Listen and put a cross by the correct ending.
Mario has:

broken his ankle. ☐
cut his ankle. ☐
sprained his ankle. ☒

– No me encuentro bien. Me duele mucho el tobillo, creo que me lo he torcido.

Listening strategies

- Make sure you are familiar with the KEY VERBS for every topic. Then if something unusual comes up (here: torcer – to sprain), you should be able to rule out the other options from your knowledge of Me he roto / cortado.

- Study the different options BEFORE you listen. Then you will be better prepared.

Now try this

LISTENING 12 **target B**

Listen to the whole recording and put a cross by the correct endings.

1 Mario hurt himself when: he was running. ☐   he was playing football. ☐   he fell off his horse. ☐
2 His ankle has been hurting since: yesterday. ☐   the day before yesterday. ☐   two days ago. ☐
3 The doctor advises Mario to: take asprin. ☐   go to hospital. ☐   rest. ☐

At the tourist office

You need to know the vocabulary for tourist attractions. Learn the genders too!

En la oficina de turismo

¿Tiene …?	Do you have …?
un mapa de la región	a map of the region
una lista de hoteles	a list of hotels
una lista de albergues de juventud	a list of youth hostels
un folleto de excursiones	a brochure about trips
un horario de trenes / autobuses	a train / bus timetable
Quisiera información sobre …	I'd like information about …
Hay …	There is …
Es posible	It's possible

¿Qué hay de interés en …?
What is there of interest in …?

Si yo fuera usted, visitaría …
If I were you, I would visit …

¿A qué hora abre / cierra el museo?
What time does the museum open / close?

Question words

Grammar page 101

¿Dónde?	Where?
¿Adónde?	Where to?
¿Cuánto?	How much?
¿Cuándo?	When?
¿A qué hora?	At what time?
¿Qué?	What?
¿Cómo?	How?
¿Cuál?	Which?

Attractions in a town

playas bonitas	beautiful beaches
museos interesantes	interesting museums
una vida nocturna animada	lively nightlife
la comida rica	tasty food

Los jardines son bonitos. The gardens are beautiful.

Worked example

SPEAKING

¿Qué hay de interés en Cádiz?

Fui a Cádiz el año pasado. Hay muchas playas bonitas y se puede comer muy bien. La gente es muy simpática y me gustaría volver.

Cádiz
- Playas bonitas
- Vida nocturna animada
- Carnavales interesantes
- Comida rica

This student has used a **variety of tenses** but the vocabulary is a little simple.

AIMING HIGHER Hay mucho que hacer en Cádiz, las playas son bonitas y además la gente es muy simpática. Fui el año pasado y lo pasé fenomenal. Es interesante ver el carnaval en febrero. Si yo fuera usted, visitaría los bares, ya que la vida nocturna es muy animada.

This answer features a selection of **complex phrases**, including:
- the preterite (**fui**)
- the conditional (**visitaría**)
- imperfect subjunctive (**si yo fuera**).

Now try this

SPEAKING

Answer the following question. Talk for one minute. The points below will give you some ideas.
Qué hay de interés en Londres?
- museos
- vida nocturna animada
- jardines
- comida

What to do in town

This page gives more town vocabulary to help with listening and reading tasks.

Actividades en la ciudad

¿Qué se puede hacer en tu ciudad?
What can you do in your town?

En (Bilbao) se puede ...	In (Bilbao) you can ...
ir al teatro	go to the theatre
ir a la catedral	go to the cathedral
ir a la piscina	go to the swimming pool
visitar los museos	visit museums
jugar en los parques	play in the parks
ver el puerto	see the port
ver un partido	see a match
ir a las corridas	go to the bullfighting

conocer la cultura
experience the culture

ver un espectáculo de flamenco
see a flamenco show

caminar por el casco antiguo
walk through the old town

ver plazas y puentes
see squares and bridges

disfrutar de unas vistas espléndidas
enjoy some wonderful views

Using se puede to say what you can do

Se puede is an impersonal verb used to talk about what people in general can do. It is followed by the infinitive.

Se puede visitar un parque temático.
You can visit a theme park.

If you are talking about more than one thing, use se pueden:

Se pueden practicar muchos deportes.
You can do many sports.

Worked example

What can you do in your town?

Mi ciudad es muy interesante. Se puede visitar el museo y además hay muchos restaurantes y bares donde se pueden comer tapas.

AIMING HIGHER Se puede visitar el museo y así se conoce la cultura. A mí me encanta Bilbao porque se puede experimentar la cultura vasca. También se puede caminar por el casco antiguo y se puede ver un espectáculo de música vasca porque forma parte de su patrimonio cultural.

Aiming higher

Try to include the following features:

- a connective (así, porque, pero, etc.) to make a complex sentence
- opinion phrases (en mi opinión, me encanta)
- less common verbs (to show a wider range of vocabulary)
- more detail (make sure it's relevant though!).

Now try this

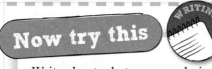

Write about what you can do in your town, in about 100 words.

Remember to use the Aiming higher advice!

Signs in town

Town signs may crop up in reading tasks – make sure you can recognise them.

Las señales

la entrada
entrance

la salida
exit

la salida de emergencia
emergency exit

la estación (de autobuses)
(bus) station

la piscina
swimming pool

el aparcamiento
car park

el cajero
cashpoint

el centro de la ciudad
town centre

los servicios
toilets

Understanding instructions

Grammar page 96

These expressions all feature in town signs. You can also use them to explain what people in general aren't allowed to do, and what's compulsory. Note that they are all followed by an INFINITIVE.

No se permite …	You are not allowed …
Está prohibido …	It is forbidden …
No se debe …	You shouldn't …
Tiene que …	You have to …
No se permite fumar.	You are not allowed to smoke.
Está prohibido aparcar.	It is forbidden to park here.

Worked example

READING   target F

Look at the signs. Who does each sign apply to? Read the sentences and draw a cross in the grid.

	Prohibido Perros	Prohibido fumar	Prohibido aparcar	Piscina	Cajero	Estación de autobuses
Pablo	x					
Teresa						
Marta						
Feliciano						
Alicia						
Rico						

a Pablo is thinking of taking his dog to the park.
b Teresa wants to go swimming.
c Marta needs to catch a bus.
d Feliciano has run out of money.
e Alicia isn't sure if she can smoke.
f Rico is looking for a parking space.

Look for any words that look like the English. For example, the third sign has **aparcar** which looks like 'parking'.

Now try this

READING   target F

Complete the activity above.

At the train station

Use this page to get ready to understand and talk about details of rail travel.

En la estación de trenes

RENFE	Spanish national rail company
la consigna	left luggage
el compartimento	compartment
llegadas / salidas	arrivals / departures
un enlace	connection
un retraso	a delay
la tarifa	the fare
la línea	the route
el andén / la vía	the platform
la sala de espera	waiting room
un coche cama	a sleeping car
el revisor	ticket inspector
la oficina de billetes	ticket office
un tren de cercanías	a local (stopping) train
hacer transbordo	to change trains
bajar / subir	to get on / get off

Talking about arriving and departing

Use llegar and salir in the perfect and future tenses to talk about arrivals and departures.

Perfect	
Ha llegado.	It has arrived.
Ha salido.	It has left.
Future	
Llegará.	It will arrive.
Saldrá.	It will leave.

El tren procedente de Madrid ha llegado.

The train from Madrid has arrived.

El tren con destino a Barcelona saldrá a las ocho.
The Barcelona train will leave at 8 o'clock.

Worked example

LISTENING 13   target D

Listen and answer the question.

Which platform has the train from Salamanca arrived at?

Platform 17

> – El tren de las catorce trienta procedente de Salamanca ha llegado al andén diecisiete.

Listening strategies

Read the questions BEFORE you start listening. Identify the key words to listen out for.

- The **key word** to recognise here is andén – otherwise, you risk picking out the wrong number.
- Make sure you know key **rail travel** vocabulary – and don't forget to revise **numbers** and **time** for this topic as well.

Now try this

LISTENING 14   target D

Listen to the whole recording and answer these questions.

1 When will the train to Seville leave?
2 Has the 3.30 from Seville already arrived?
3 What does he say about the next train from Madrid?

Weather

There are usually lots of opportunities to add a weather phrase in your writing and speaking assessments. Don't forget to use a range of tenses, too!

El tiempo

Llueve / Está lloviendo.   Nieva / Está nevando.

Hace sol.   Hay niebla.

Hace calor.   Hace frío.

Hace viento.	It's windy.
el pronóstico del tiempo	weather forecast
el clima	the climate
Hace mal / buen tiempo.	It's bad / good weather.
Está nublado.	It's cloudy.
Hay tormenta.	It's stormy.
seco	dry
lluvioso	rainy

Different tenses

Understanding the weather in different tenses is a higher-level skill.

Expressions with hacer	
Hacía calor.	It was hot.
Hará frío.	It will be cold.
Hará sol.	It will be sunny.
Expressions with estar	
Estaba nublado.	It was cloudy.
Expressions with haber	
Había niebla.	It was foggy.
Habrá tormenta.	It will be stormy.
nevar (to snow) and llover (to rain)	
Nevaba.	It was snowing.
Llovía.	It was raining.
Va a nevar / llover.	It's going to snow / rain.

Look out for time markers as a clue to the tense.

ayer	yesterday
hoy	today
mañana	tomorrow

Worked example

LISTENING 15 **target C**

Listen and put a cross by the correct word.

The forecast for Bilbao today is:

sun. ☒
rain. ☐
snow. ☐

— Bilbao, sábado 12 de marzo. Ayer llovía pero hoy hace sol. Mañana nevará.

EXAM ALERT!

Some candidates make errors because they haven't learned key vocabulary like time expressions. These are crucial in many situations and contexts.

Students have struggled with exam questions similar to this – **be prepared!**

The key word to listen out for here is **hoy** (today).

Now try this

LISTENING 16 **target C**

Listen to the rest of the recording and put a cross by the correct words.

1 Tomorrow it will snow in: Seville. ☐ Bilbao. ☐ both cities. ☐
2 In Seville yesterday it was: windy. ☐ cold. ☐ foggy. ☐
3 In Seville now it is: hot. ☐ stormy. ☐ cold. ☐

It will also help you if you recognise the **tenses** used. Make sure you know **hacer, estar** and **haber** in the imperfect, present and future tenses.

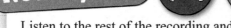

Places in a town

You need to know places in town and prepositions in order to give and understand directions.

En la ciudad

el centro comercial	shopping centre
la agencia de viajes	travel agency
la oficina de turismo	tourist office
la peluquería	hairdresser
el mercado	market
el restaurante	restaurant
las tiendas	shops
la oficina de correos	post office
el ayuntamiento	town hall
la comisaría	police station
el polideportivo	sports centre
la piscina	swimming pool
el colegio/el instituto	school
el museo de arte	art gallery
la pista de patinaje	ice rink
la biblioteca	library
la discoteca	night club
el teatro	theatre
el zoo	zoo

'I go' in different tenses

voy	I go (present)
fui	I went (preterite)
iba	I used to go (imperfect)
iré	I will go (future)
he ido	I have been (perfect)

Prepositions

Use prepositions to describe location.
Note that de + el changes to del.

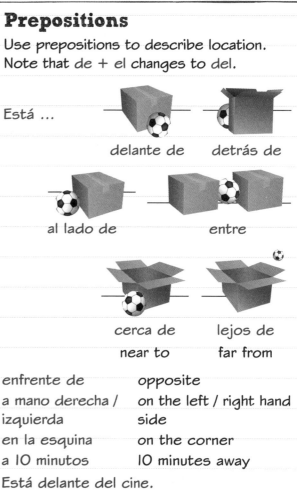

Está ...

delante de   detrás de

al lado de   entre

cerca de   lejos de
near to   far from

enfrente de	opposite
a mano derecha / izquierda	on the left / right hand side
en la esquina	on the corner
a 10 minutos	10 minutes away

Está delante del cine.
It's in front of the cinema.

Worked example

 17 target C

Listen and answer the question.
Where did Luisa go yesterday? library

– ¡Hola, Luisa! ¿Dónde fuiste ayer?
– Iba a ir a las tiendas pero al final fui a la biblioteca para estudiar para el examen.

Listening strategies

- Remember to listen to the END of what someone says. If you thought you'd got the answer from the first part (a las tiendas), you'd be wrong!
- Listen carefully to VERBS to try and work out the correct tense (Iba a ir – I was going to go).
- Listen for CLUE WORDS, e.g. al final (which here indicates a change of plan).

Now try this

 18 target C

Listen to the whole recording and answer these questions.

Don't be distracted by redundant details like **Voy al teatro**. Focus on the questions.

1 Where is the library located?
2 Where did Ignacio go yesterday?
3 Where is the disco?

Where I live

Use this page to talk about the advantages and disadvantages of where you live.

Mi barrio

Lo bueno es que ...	The good thing is ...
Es interesante.	It's interesting.
Es tranquilo.	It's peaceful.
Hay vistas bonitas.	There are beautiful views.
Hay mucho que hacer.	There's a lot to do.

Hay muchas diversiones para los jóvenes.
There are lots of attractions for young people.

La gente es acogedora.
The people are welcoming.

Lo malo es que ...	The bad thing is ...
Hay contaminación.	There's pollution.
Es rudioso.	It's noisy.
Hay mucho turismo.	There's a lot of tourism.
Hay demasiado tráfico.	There's too much traffic.
el desempleo	unemployment

lo + adjective

Use lo + adjective to refer to an abstract idea.

lo bueno	the good thing
lo malo	the bad thing
lo aburrido	the boring thing
lo interesante	the interesting thing

There is also a superlative form:

Lo más interesante es que hay playas bonitas.

The most interesting thing is the beautiful beaches.

Aiming higher

Using haber in THREE TENSES will help you give a good answer.

Hay	There is (present tense)
Había	There used to be (imperfect past)
Habrá	There will be (future)

Worked example SPEAKING

¿Qué piensas de tu pueblo?

Lo que más me gusta de mi pueblo es que es tranquilo y hay muchas playas bonitas. Antes había mucho turismo y mucha contaminación.

AIMING HIGHER
Me encanta mi ciudad, vivo en Birmingham desde hace once años. Es un poco ruidoso y hay demasiado tráfico pero lo que más me gusta es que hay muchas tiendas a donde puedo ir con mis amigos. Antes vivía en un pequeño pueblo en el campo pero no me gustaba porque no había nada para los jóvenes. En el futuro me gustaría vivir en Londres.

CONTROLLED ASSESSMENT

- Presentations should last for at least **one** minute. Presentations under one minute will not earn you a higher grade, however accurate and interesting they are.
- Remember to think of some **questions** of your own to ask.

Extended sequences of speech using a variety of vocabulary (contaminación, diversiones), structures (Lo que más me gusta) and verb tenses (había, habrá) improve the answer further

Now try this SPEAKING

Remember to include **reasons** and **opinions** to make your presentation more interesting.

Answer this question.
- ¿Qué piensas de tu pueblo?

Town description

This page will help you describe your town and talk about what things you would like to change there.

Descripción de mi ciudad

Mi ciudad se llama ...	My town is called ...
Está en el norte / este / sur / oeste de Inglaterra.	It is in the north / east / south / west of England.
Hay doce mil habitantes.	There are 12,000 inhabitants.
En mi ciudad hay muchos turistas.	In my town there are lots of tourists.
muchas áreas de ocio	lots of leisure areas
una buena red de transporte público	a good public transport network
mucha contaminación	lots of pollution
muchos árboles	lots of trees
pocas tiendas de ropa	few clothes shops
pocas instalaciones	few facilities

En mi ciudad hay muchos espacios verdes.
In my town there are lots of green spaces.

Conditional

Grammar page 94

You use the conditional to talk about what you WOULD do. To form it, add the following endings to the infinitive. The endings are the same for all infinitives.

	hablar – to speak
I	hablaría
you	hablarías
he / she / it	hablaría
we	hablaríamos
you	hablaríais
they	hablarían

Construiría ...	I would build ...
Podría ...	I would be able to ...
Habría ...	There would be ...
Mejoraría ...	I would improve ...

Worked example LISTENING 19 target C

Listen and put a cross in the **four** correct boxes.

1 There are 60,000 inhabitants in Gandia. ☐
2 Gandia is in the south-east of Spain. ☒
3 Héctor would encourage more tourists to come to Gandia. ☐
4 He would provide more green spaces. ☐
5 Lanzarote does not attract tourists. ☐
6 Lanzarote is near Africa. ☐
7 There are enough buses in Lanzarote. ☐
8 Laura thinks more buses wouldn't make life better. ☐

– Vivo en Gandia, una ciudad que tiene más de setenta mil habitantes.

Listening strategies

- ALWAYS read the options before you listen. Identify key words and structures to listen for.
- If you are sure of any answers on first listening, cross the boxes and cross out the sentence to reduce your options.

Look at the sentences. What do you need to listen out for?
- Numbers (sesenta? – no: setenta)
- Prepositions (en África? – no: cerca de África)
- Verbs in the conditional.
- Key words like turistas, autobuses, espacios verdes, etc.

Now try this LISTENING 20 target C

Listen to the whole recording and complete the activity by finding the other **three** correct sentences.

Holiday destinations

Use this page to talk about holidays and to compare different tourist destinations.

Dónde ir de vacaciones

Me gusta ir ...	I like to go ...
a la montaña	to the mountain
a la playa	to the beach
a nuestro piso de España	to our flat in Spain
a ver a nuestra familia	to see our family
a lugares exóticos	to exotic places
a sitios culturales	to cultural places
Soy muy deportista.	I'm very sporty.
donde puedo practicar el español	where I can practise my Spanish
Es más relajante / tranquilo.	It's more relaxing / peaceful.
Hay menos gente.	It's less busy.
Está menos contaminado.	It's less polluted.

Las vacaciones con aventuras son más emocionante que ir a la costa.
Adventure holidays are more exciting than going to the coast.

Making comparisons

Grammar page 84

Use the comparative to compare two places or holidays, identifying differences and similarities.

más	+ adjective + que = more ... than
menos	+ adjective + que = less ... than
tan	+ adjective + como = as ... as

Madrid es menos interesante que Barcelona.

Madrid is less interesting than Barcelona.

Worked example

Say what kind of holiday you prefer.

Normalmente vamos a nuestro piso de España, está en la costa y puedo ir a pie a las playas. A mis padres les gusta la cultura, por eso este año vamos a Florencia – va a ser muy aburrido.

AIMING HIGHER
Me gusta ir a la montaña, a Italia, a esquiar. Es más interesante que la playa. Antes me gustaba ir a la playa pero hoy en día soy más deportista y por eso me encantan las vacaciones con aventuras. En el futuro me gustaría ir a un lugar exótico.

Writing strategies

- Plan out what you want to say BEFORE you start writing. Make short notes, including key phrases to include.
- Leave time to CHECK over what you've written. Check endings on adjectives and verbs in particular.

- The accurate use of the comparative (**es más interesante**) shows the ability to produce longer, fluent sentences with ease.
- The connective **y por eso** is also an impressive inclusion.
- Using **gustar** in three different tenses (**me gusta, me gustaba, me gustaría**) shows a confident use of more complex structures.

Now try this

Say what kind of holiday you prefer. Write about 200 words.
- Compare it with other types of holiday.
- Include details of previous holidays.
- Say where you would like to go in the future.

Try to use different forms of **gustar** and include two **comparative** sentences.

Holiday accommodation

Use this page to talk more about your holidays and to express your holiday preferences.

El alojamiento

Estoy en ...	I stay in ...
Me alojo en ...	I stay in ...
un camping	a campsite
un hotel de cinco estrellas	a five-star hotel
un albergue de juventud	a youth hostel
una pensión / un hostal	a guest house
nuestro apartamento de Francia	our flat in France
alquilar	to hire, rent
una caravana	a caravan
un piso alquilado	a rented flat
una casa	a house
Prefiero quedarme en un hotel.	I prefer staying in a hotel.

Using me gusta(n) and me encanta(n)

> Grammar page 99

Me gusta (I like) literally translates as 'it pleases me'. The thing that does the pleasing (i.e. the thing I like) is the subject. If this subject is plural, use me gustan. Me encanta behaves in the same way.

Me gusta dormir al aire libre.
I like sleeping outdoors.

Me encanta alquilar un apartamento.
I love renting a flat.

And to say what you don't like ...

No me gusta quedarme en un camping.
I don't like staying on a campsite.

me gusta ♥
me gusta mucho ♥ ♥
me encanta ♥ ♥ ♥

Aiming higher

Using quedarse as well as alojarse in the PRETERITE and FUTURE will improve your knowledge of language marks.

me quedé / me alojé	I stayed
me quedaré / me alojaré	I will stay

Worked example

SPEAKING

¿Dónde prefieres alojarte?

AIMING HIGHER Normalmente, voy a un camping bastante aburrido pero el año pasado me quedé en un hotel precioso de cinco estrellas. El año que viene, voy a ir a un parador de lujo. Prefiero quedarme en un hotel porque no me gusta dormir al aire libre. Me encantan los hoteles lujosos.

Speaking strategies

- Use a mental checklist whenever you are preparing for a speaking exam. Think: * CONNECTIVES * ADJECTIVES * TENSES

- CONNECTIVES are easy to use to combine two short sentences with y or pero.

- ADJECTIVES make your speaking and writing much more interesting: memorise a good range of them (aburrido boring, precioso beautiful, de lujo luxury), etc.

- TENSES should be shown off! Think PPF (present, past, future). How can you incorporate all three into your answer?

Now try this

SPEAKING

Look at the photo above. Talk for one minute about it. Give your opinion.

Staying in a hotel

Be prepared to talk in detail about where you stay on holiday.

En un hotel

Quisiera reservar ...	I'd like to reserve ...
una habitación individual / doble	a single / double room
sin baño	without a bathroom
con ducha / balcón	with a shower / balcony
¿Para cuántas noches?	For how many nights?
para siete noches	for seven nights
¿A qué hora sirven el desayuno / la cena?	What time is breakfast / dinner served?
¿Está incluido el desayuno?	Is breakfast included?
completo	full
con vistas al mar / a la piscina / a las montañas	with a sea / pool / mountain view
la recepción	reception
la llave	key
el ascensor	lift
media pensión	half board
pensión completa	full board
conexión a Internet	internet connection
quince días	fortnight

Revising numbers

Grammar page 103

You can never review numbers too often! Here are a few ideas:

- LOOK AT the numbers on page 103. Can you identify any patterns that will help you remember them?
  - 16 to 19 are dieci + 6, dieci + 7, etc.
  - 31, 41, 51, etc. are always y uno (but 21 is different)
  - tres / trece / treinta
- PLAY BINGO with friends. Agree on 12 numbers you all find difficult to distinguish (e.g. cinco / quince, ocho / ochenta). One person is the caller; the others choose and write four of the numbers each. The caller reads out the numbers in random order until one of you has checked them all off – Bingo!
- PRACTISE numbers on your own: count in twos, in threes, in fives. Count backwards!

Worked example

LISTENING 21   target C

Listen and put a cross in the **four** correct boxes.

1 Carolina wants a double room. ☒
2 She would like a sea view. ☐
3 She wants to stay for two weeks. ☐
4 The price is 360€. ☐
5 Mateo wants to stay for ten nights. ☐
6 He does not want breakfast. ☐
7 He wants full board. ☐
8 The price is 460€. ☐

– Hotel Sol. ¿Dígame?
– Quisiera reservar una habitación doble con baño y con vistas a la piscina.

Work out which numbers you're going to listen out for. That will help you identify the tricky ones.

EXAM ALERT!

Numbers have frequently come up in listening texts so make sure you learn them well. Be careful not to muddle numbers that are a bit similar, though.

This was a real exam question that a lot of students struggled with – **be prepared!**

 ResultsPlus

Now try this

LISTENING 22   target C

Listen to the whole recording and complete the activity by finding the other three correct sentences.

Staying on a campsite

Learn the vocabulary here to help you understand a text on rules and regulations.

En un camping

¿Se puede acampar aquí?	Can I camp here?
las normas / las reglas	the rules
una tienda / caravana	a tent / caravan
hacer fuego	to light a fire
una toma de corriente	an electricity point
la lavandería	laundry
las duchas	the showers
un saco de dormir	sleeping bag
el gas butano	camping gas
agua potable	drinking water
Es obligatorio	It is compulsory

Quisiera una parcela para dos noches.
I'd like a pitch for two nights.

hacer una barbacoa
to have a barbecue

No se permite hacer ruido.
Being noisy is not allowed.

No se permiten animales.
Animals are not allowed.

Note: Use **se permite** if it refers to a single thing, but **se permiten** if it refers to more than one thing.

Using different verbs

To make your writing and speaking more varied, don't just use different tenses – use different verbs too. Make lists in diagrams like this:

- ir — to go
- llegar — to arrive
- conducir — to drive
- entrar — to enter
- visitar — to visit
- VERBS OF MOVEMENT
- caminar — to walk
- venir — to come
- salir — to leave
- volver — to return
- dejar — to leave
- pasar por — to pass by, go through

Worked example

READING · target C

Read the texts.

En el camping
- El horario de silencio es de 01:00h a 07:00h y se prohíbe la circulación de vehículos.
- No se permite hacer carreras con bicicletas.
- Están prohibidos los juegos de pelota cerca de las tiendas.
- El volumen o sonido de los aparatos de televisión debe ser, durante todo el día, lo más bajo posible.

En el albergue de juventud
- No se permite hacer ruido después de medianoche.
- No se permite comer en los dormitorios.
- Es obligatorio tener tu propio saco de dormir.
- Es obligatorio utilizar los cubos para basura.

Which of these sentences is correct?

In the campsite ...

You can drive your car at 8.00 am. ☒

You can have bicycle races. ☐

EXAM ALERT!

Students perform well in tasks like this when they have a good knowledge of basic vocabulary items and use deductive reasoning. Use your ability to think, as well as your knowledge of Spanish!

This was a real exam question that a lot of students struggled with – **be prepared!**

ResultsPlus

Now try this

READING · target C

Put a cross in the **three** correct boxes.

In the campsite ...

1 You can play ball games. ☐

2 You can play your television loudly. ☐

In the youth hostel ...

3 You mustn't be noisy after midday. ☐

4 You mustn't eat in the dormitories. ☐

5 You must have your own sleeping bag. ☐

6 You must take your rubbish away with you. ☐

Holiday preferences

This page will help you express your opinion in lots of different ways.

Prefiero las vacaciones ...

🙂

🙁

Prefiero las vacaciones en la playa con amigos.
I prefer holidays on the beach with friends.
Mis vacaciones ideales serían en el Caribe.
My ideal holidays would be in the Caribbean.
Es maravilloso conocer una ciudad y perderme por las calles estrechas.
It's wonderful getting to know a city and losing myself in the narrow streets.
Siempre he querido visitar Australia.
I have always wanted to visit Australia.
Es relajante descansar sin pensar en el instituto.
It's relaxing to take it easy without thinking about school.

No me gusta ir de vacaciones con mis padres.
I don't like going on holiday with my parents.
No soporto hacer camping.
I can't stand going camping.
Odio los sitios arruinados por el turismo descontrolado.
I hate places ruined by uncontrolled tourism.
Me da vergüenza el comportamiento de los británicos.
British holidaymakers make me ashamed.
Odio el sol porque siempre me pongo rojo.
I hate the sun as it always makes me red.
Me aburren los museos y la historia.
Museums and history bore me.

Worked example

WRITING

Talk about your preferred holiday destination.

Mis vacaciones ideales serían en España. Primero, diría que las vacaciones en España sin padres son fenomenales pero ellos pagan todo, así que con padres no están tan mal.

- This question allows use of the **conditional** to say what your favourite type of holiday would be.
- A **time phrase** (primero) and a **connective** (pero) make this answer flow well.

AIMING HIGHER

Mis vacaciones ideales serían en Italia. Podría visitar las ciudades famosas como Florencia y Roma. Me apasionan el arte y los museos. Además, la comida es maravillosa. Creó que tardaré muchos años en ir a Italia porque a mis padres le gusta el sol, así que tenemos que ir a la playa como todos los británicos ¡me da tanta vergüenza su comportamiento!

This answer includes a variety of tenses and complex phrases (**me da vergüenza**). It also expresses different opinions.

Aiming higher

Try to include MORE COMPLEX language.
Mis padres siempre quieren que vaya con ellos.
My parents always want me to go with them.
Si pudiera, iría a Ibiza para ir de fiesta.
If I could, I'd go to Ibiza to party.

Now try this

WRITING

Write about your preferred holiday destination in about 100 words.

- Refer to different options you have thought about, considering the pros and cons.
- Talk about holidays you have already had.
- Include opinions.

Holiday activities

Be prepared to talk about a wide range of activities that you enjoy doing on holiday.

Las actividades de vacaciones

¿Qué haces normalmente cuando estás de vacaciones?
What do you normally do on holiday?
Voy con mi familia / mis amigos.
I go with my family / friends.

Descanso / me relajo.	I relax.
Saco fotos.	I take photos.
Pinto y dibujo.	I paint and I draw.

Learning vocabulary

- Make yourself FLASHCARDS to help you memorise vocabulary – Spanish on one side and English (or a picture) on the other.
- Write NOTECARDS to help you prepare for assessments – write key words and phrases, structures and verb forms under topic headings.

Me baño en el mar.

Voy a discotecas.

Hago excursiones.

Hago esquí.

Hago surfing.

Hago piragüismo.

Monto en bicicleta.

Worked example

SPEAKING

¿Qué haces normalmente cuando estás de vacaciones?

Voy a Portugal con mis amigos. Es divertido porque vamos a discotecas. Nunca voy con mis padres porque es un rollo.

AIMING HIGHER Siempre voy de vacaciones con mi hermana. Tiene dos años más que yo, por lo que tenemos los mismos gustos. El año pasado fuimos a Ibiza. ¡Fue estupendo! Nos bañamos en el mar y descansamos en la playa. Por las noches íbamos a las discotecas y bailábamos hasta las tres de la mañana. Yo creo que a mis padres les gustaría que fuéramos con ellos pero sería aburrido.

Speaking strategies

- Students who use a lot of words which are the same in English will only impress if they PRONOUNCE them in the correct Spanish way.
- Make sure you've learned a GOOD RANGE of vocabulary – filling a presentation with English words is not a good idea.

Now try this

SPEAKING

Answer this question. Talk for about one minute.

- ¿Qué haces normalmente cuando estás de vacaciones?

Review the **present tense** (see page 87) to prepare yourself for this topic. Don't just revise 'I' forms – be ready to talk about what your friends and family do on holiday, too, and what you do together.

Booking accommodation

Use this page to revise booking accommodation vocabulary for your listening and reading exams.

Reservar habitaciones

Estimado señor	Dear Sir
Quisiera reservar	I'd like to reserve
Pensamos quedarnos	We are thinking of staying
para una semana	for one week
desde el 6 hasta el 9 de enero	from 6 to 9 January
por la tarde	in the afternoon / evening
Somos cuatro.	There are four of us.
Le ruego que me mande	Please send me
Vamos a llegar a …	We are going to arrive at …
Le saluda atentamente	Yours faithfully
Gracias por su ayuda	Thanks for your help
Agradeciéndole de antemano su ayuda	
Thanks in advance for your help	
¿Cuánto cuesta?	
How much does it cost?	
con balcón y con vistas al mar	
with a balcony and sea view	

Using para and por for 'for'

Grammar page 100

Use these rules to work out whether to use para or por.

POR – cause
Gracias por su ayuda. Thanks for your help.
POR – expressing rates
Son 50 euros por noche. It's 50 euros per night.
PARA – purpose
Voy a utilizar mi tarjeta de crédito para pagar. I'm going to use my credit card to pay.
PARA – a destination
Salió para Granada. He has left for Granada.
PARA – period of time in the future
Quiero una habitación para una semana. I would like a room for a week.

Worked example WRITING

Write an email to book a hotel.

AIMING HIGHER

Estimado señor,
Quisiera reservar una habitación para quince días para mi familia. Somos cinco personas y vamos a llegar el 15 de agosto por la tarde. La fecha de salida es el 29 de agosto.
Quisiera, si es posible, habitaciones con balcón y vistas al mar. Le ruego que me comunique el precio total y me mande un correo de confirmación.
Agradeciéndole de antemano su ayuda.
Le saluda atentamente.

Make sure you use formal expressions as you would in English. Try to memorise the key phrases Spanish people use in writing letters of this sort.

Learning strategies

Try this to help you memorise the formal expressions:

WRITE each one in big writing and cut out the words. SHUFFLE them, then put them in order – do this several times until you're confident. Then try to write out the complete expressions WITHOUT looking at the cut-out words.

Now try this WRITING

Write an e-mail of about 100 words to book a holiday.

- Say you want to stay for two weeks.
- Say it is for four people.
- Say when you will arrive / depart.
- Ask about prices and meals.

Try to include a request for a particular requirement.

Future holiday plans

Make sure you know the future tense to talk about your holiday plans.

Vacaciones en el futuro

Nos quedaremos en un hotel.	We will stay in a hotel.
Iré ...	I will go ...
a la costa	to the coast
a la montaña	to the mountains
a la playa	to the beach
al campo	to the country
Descansaré.	I will rest.
Nadaré.	I will swim.
Haré yoga.	I will do yoga.
Iré a clases de baile.	I will go to dance classes.
Daré una vuelta en bicicleta.	I will go on a cycling tour.
Veré lugares de interés.	I will see places of interest.
Montaré a caballo.	I will go horseriding.
Patinaré.	I will skate.
Esquiaré.	I will ski.
Haré alpinismo.	I will go rock climbing.
Haré vela.	I will go sailing.

Future tense

Grammar page 93

To form the future tense of most verbs, add the following endings to the infinitive:

	ir – to go
I go	iré
you go	iras
he / she / it goes	irá
we go	iremos
you go	iréis
they go	irán

¿Adónde irás de vacaciones el año que viene?

Where will you go on holiday next year?

Iré a Grecia y daré una vuelta en bicicleta. I'll go to Greece and I'll go on a cycling tour.

Worked example

WRITING

Say where you will go on holiday next year.

Esquiaré en Francia con mi instituto. Va a ser genial. Nos quedaremos en un hotel cerca de las montañas.

AIMING HIGHER

El año que viene iré a la costa de Italia con mi novio. Creo que va a ser perfecto porque serán nuestras primera vacaciones juntos. Descansaremos en la playa, y mi novio dará una vuelta en bicicleta. A mi me encantan los caballos asi que montaré en caballo cada día.

Using the **future** and the **near future** shows variety of tense usage.

Adding more **detail** (where you will stay) can improve the content.

- Extending opinions by justifying them using **connectives** (y, porque) will help you if you are aiming higher.
- You can also use **interesting phrases** to show your grasp of a wider range of vocabulary, e.g. **nuestras primeras vacaciones juntos** (our first holiday together).

Now try this

WRITING

- Say where you will go on holiday next year. Write about 150 words. Mention:
  - the destination
  - who you will go with and for how long
  - what you will do
  - what it will be like and why.

Past holidays

Past holidays is a popular topic in the exam. Make sure you've revised the appropriate verb forms.

Vacaciones pasadas

¿Adónde fuiste de vacaciones el año pasado?
Where did you go on holiday last year?

el verano pasado	last summer
hace dos años	two years ago
Fui ...	I went ...
con mi familia / mis solo	with my family / alone
Me alojé/Me quedé ...	I stayed ...
Viajé en ...	I travelled by ...
Hice un intercambio.	I did an exchange.
Pasé una semana allí.	I spent one week there.
Hice un viaje escolar.	I went on a school trip.

Fui con mis amigos.   I went with my friends.

Preterite tense

Grammar page 91

These verbs in the preterite will be useful for talking about past holidays.

	visitar – to visit	comer – to eat	salir – to go out
I	visité	comí	salí
you	visitaste	comiste	saliste
he / she / it	visitó	comió	salió
we	visitamos	comimos	salimos
you	visitasteis	comisteis	salisteis
they	visitaron	comieron	salieron

Useful verbs in the preterite for talking about holidays include:

vi	I saw
bebí	I drank
hice	I did
fue	it was
tuve	I had

Bebí un zumo de naranja.

Worked example   SPEAKING

¿Adónde fuiste de vacaciones el año pasado?

El verano pasado me quedé en mi pueblo. Fue bastante divertido porque vi a mis primos de Estado Unidos. Jugamos al fútbol cada día y montamos en bicicleta.

AIMING HIGHER

El verano pasado fui a Marruecos. Pasé dos semanas allí y fue una experiencia estupenda. Viajé en avión pero lo peor fue que el vuelo duró tres horas y fue muy aburrido así que la próxima vez me quedaré en Inglaterra.

CONTROLLED ASSESSMENT

- Your speaking assessment should last between 4 and 6 minutes. Students who speak for only 3 minutes will not get the higher grades. Examiners stop listening after 6 minutes, so anything said after that time is not marked.

- If you're asked an open question, don't panic! Use the strategies you have learned to help you structure your response. Learning chunks of language before the exam will also give you confidence – you'll find that you can use them in all sorts of language situations.

Including opinions will make your speaking more interesting.
Lo peor fue ...   The worst thing was ...
Lo mejor fue ...   The best thing was ...

Now try this   SPEAKING

Prepare your answer to the following question. Speak for about one minute.

- ¿Adónde fuiste de vacaciones el año pasado?

Directions

Learn the key vocabulary here to understand directions and revise the imperative in order to give them.

Las direcciones

¿Dónde está ...?   Where is ...?
¿Por dónde se va a ...?   How do you get to ...?

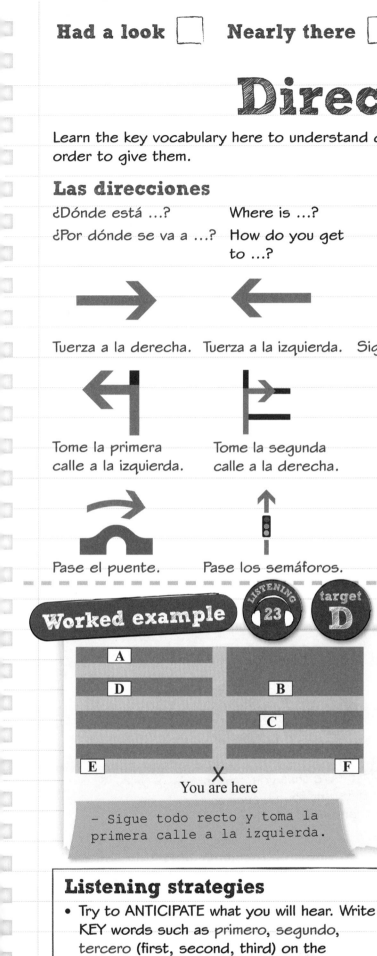

Tuerza a la derecha.   Tuerza a la izquierda.   Siga todo recto.

Tome la primera calle a la izquierda.   Tome la segunda calle a la derecha.

Pase el puente.   Pase los semáforos.

la tercera calle   the third road
Doble la esquina.   Turn the corner.
Cruce la plaza.   Cross the square.

Giving instructions

> Grammar page 96

Use the IMPERATIVE to give instructions. There are two forms, depending on whether you are talking to a friend (informal) or a stranger (formal).

informal	formal	
sigue	siga	follow
tuerce	tuerza	turn
cruza	cruce	cross
toma	tome	take

Worked example 🎧 23 target D

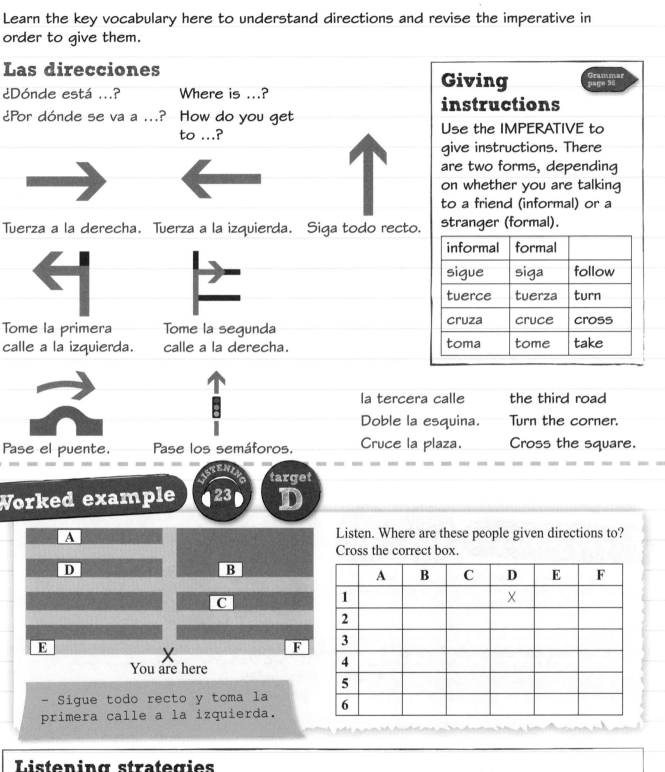

You are here

– Sigue todo recto y toma la primera calle a la izquierda.

Listen. Where are these people given directions to? Cross the correct box.

	A	B	C	D	E	F
1				X		
2						
3						
4						
5						
6						

Listening strategies

- Try to ANTICIPATE what you will hear. Write KEY words such as primero, segundo, tercero (first, second, third) on the appropriate part of the map to help you.

- Listen for key direction verbs. Here, it doesn't matter if they're formal or informal – you just need to recognise the verb.

Now try this 🎧 24 target D

Listen to the rest of the recording and complete the activity.

Transport

Use this vocabulary to understand and talk about how people get around.

El transporte

en coche   en tren   en barco   en metro   en moto

en autobús   en autocar   en bicicleta   en avión   a pie

- Note cojo – I catch.
- el for all transport except la bicicleta/ la moto.
- en coche (by car), etc., but a pie (on foot)

Es ...	It's ...		
limpio	clean	Viajo en avión.	I travel by plane.
sucio	dirty	Prefiero coger el autobús.	I prefer to catch the bus.
cómodo	comfortable	Odio ir andando.	I hate walking.
incómodo	uncomfortable	lentamente	slowly
lento	slow	generalmente	generally
rápido	fast	normalmente	normally
barato	cheap	rápidamente	quickly
caro	expensive	frecuentemente	frequently

mejor para el ambiente medio
better for the environment

Worked example LISTENING 25 target D

Listen. How does this person travel, and why?

	Mode of transport	Reason
Ex	car	hates walking

– Normalmente voy en coche porque odio ir andando.

Make sure that you can recognise verbs in different forms, such as the gerund, e.g. **andando** (walking).

Now try this LISTENING 26 target D

Listen to the rest of the recording and complete the table.

	Mode of transport	Reason
1		
2		
3		
4		

Buying tickets

As well as revising ticket vocabulary, make sure you know your numbers for times and prices.

Comprar billetes

Quiero dos billetes para …	I would like two tickets to …
un billete de ida	a single ticket
un billete de ida y vuelta	a return ticket
para hoy / mañana	for today / tomorrow
¿A qué hora sale / llega?	What times does it depart / arrive?
Es directo.	It's direct.
un bonobús	a ticket for 10 trips
no fumador	non smoking
¿Cuánto cuesta?	How much does it cost?
¿Hay un descuento para los jóvenes?	Is there a discount for young people?
¿Cuánto tiempo dura el viaje?	How long does the journey take?
Dura …	It takes …
el próximo / último tren	the next / last train
acabar de llegar / salir	to have just arrived / left

The 24-hour clock

The 24-hour clock is often used to talk about travel times.

 las nueve treinta

 las doce cuarenta y cinco

 las dieciséis quince

 las diecinueve cero cinco

 las veinte catorce

 las veintitrés

Worked example
LISTENING 27 · **target D**

Listen and put a cross by the correct ending.
The man wants …
a single ticket. ☒
a ticket to Valencia. ☐
a ticket for tomorrow. ☐

– Quiero un billete de ida para Sevilla para hoy.

Now try this
LISTENING 28 · **target D**

Listen and put a cross by the correct ending.

1 The man's train will leave at … 14.50. ☐ 15.40. ☐ 16.50. ☐
2 The woman wants a ticket for … today. ☐ tomorrow. ☐ the end of the week. ☐
3 The woman's ticket costs … 13 euros. ☐ 67 euros. ☐ 79 euros. ☐

Eating tapas

Learn these food words with their definite articles. Then you'll always know the gender.

Comer tapas

Quiero probar ...	I'd like to try ...
el chorizo	chorizo
el gazpacho	cold soup
el jamón	ham
la paella	paella
la tortilla española	Spanish omelette
las albóndigas	meatballs
las gambas al ajillo	garlic prawns
las aceitunas	olives
Era bueno/a.	It was tasty.
Son ricos/as.	They're tasty.
Eran picantes.	They were spicy.

The definite article

Grammar page 81

The definite article (the) changes to match the gender and number of the noun.

	Singular	Plural
Masculine	el gazpacho	los calamares
Feminine	la paella	las gambas

Using the definite article with me gusta

When me gusta / me encanta is used with a noun, you need the definite article:

Me gusta el jamón.	I like ham.
Me gustan las albóndigas.	I like meatballs.
No me gustó nada el chorizo.	I hated the chorizo.
Me encantaron los churros.	I loved the churros.

Worked example WRITING

Give your opinion about a meal you had on holiday.

Me encantó la comida española. Cuando estuve en Madrid cominos tapas, todo era muy sabrosa. Me gustaron mucho las albóndigas y el jamón.

Expanding your answer by saying exactly what you ate and including an opinion will help add interest. Always give as much **detail** as you can.

AIMING HIGHER El año pasado fui a San Sebastián, la ciudad de los pinchos – 'las tapas'. Cada tarde probamos varios tipos de pinchos , incluso las gambas al ajillo, los boquerones y mucho más. Sin embargo, no me gustaron nada las patatas bravas porque eran picantes. La próxima vez, probaré la paella porque iré a Valencia.

- The **future** tense can be used to add detail, e.g. what food you will try next time.
- Working **three tenses** into your writing will help you aim for a higher grade.

Now try this WRITING

Write 60 words about a time when you tried Spanish food – it could have been in your local tapas restaurant!

- Include past tense **opinion** verbs.
- Add **details** of what you ate.
- Try to include **three tenses**.

Eating in a café

Make sure you revise plenty of food words – they can be used in lots of contexts!

Comer en la cafetería

¿Qué va a tomar?	What would you like?
Voy a tomar ...	I'll have ...
agua con gas	sparkling mineral water
agua sin gas	still mineral water
un café (solo)	a black coffee
una limonada	a lemonade
un té	a tea
un zumo de naranja	an orange juice
con azúcar	with sugar
con leche	with milk
con / sin hielo	with / without ice
un bocadillo	a sandwich
una hamburguesa	hamburger
un helado	an ice cream
un perrito caliente	a hot dog
un vaso	a glass
una botella	a bottle
una taza	a cup

High frequency words

Watch out for key but easily-overlooked words that affect meaning.

café con azúcar	coffee with sugar
café sin azúcar	coffee without sugar
nunca	never
siempre	always
solo	only
hasta	until
todo el mundo	everybody
salvo / excepto	except
a causa de	because of

En mi familia todo el mundo bebe té sin leche.
In my family everyone drinks tea without milk.

Siempre meriendo galletas.
I always snack on biscuits.

Worked example

 READING · target C

Read the text.

Ana: No voy a las cafeterías porque los helados nunca son baratos. Prefiero tomar un té con amigos en mi casa.

Pablo: Siempre voy a una cafetería con amigos para tomar un café y charlar con ellos. También comemos helados.

Miguel: Voy a la cafetería con mis hijos pero solamente los fines de semana. Mis hijos siempre comen el mismo helado: un helado de chocolate.

María: Como todo el mundo va a la cafetería, prefiero quedar con mis amigos en mi casa para tomar un té o café ya que es más tranquilo. Además, odio los helados.

Write the correct names to answer the questions.

1 Who finds ice cream cafés sociable places?
Pablo

2 Who finds ice cream cafés noisy?
....

3 Who finds ice cream cafés good for children?
....

4 Who finds ice cream cafés expensive?
....

Think and **make connections.** The text may not feature the Spanish for the exact words in the question, e.g. Ana doesn't say **caro** – she says **nunca ... baratos**. Pablo says **amigos** and **charlar** – you need to make the link between this and 'sociable'.

Now try this

READING · target C

Read the text again and answer questions 2–4.

43

Eating in a restaurant

Use this vocabulary to talk about eating out in a restaurant.

Comer en el restaurante

el plato del día	dish of the day
el menú del día	set meal
la especialidad	speciality
la carta / el menú	menu
la cuenta	the bill
De primer plato ...	For the first course ...
De segundo plato ...	For the second course ...
De postre ...	For dessert ...
Para beber ...	To drink ...
Quiero ...	I want ...
una ensalada mixta	mixed salad
una sopa de ajo	garlic soup
pescado frito	fried fish
pollo asado	roast chicken
fruta del tiempo	seasonal fruit
un flan casero	a home-made crème caramel
pan y vino	bread and wine
¡Que aproveche!	Enjoy your meal!

Using beber and comer in the preterite

	beber – to drink	comer – to eat
I	bebí	comí
he / she / it	bebió	comió
we	bebimos	comimos
they	bebieron	comieron

Comimos en un restaurante para celebrar mi cumpleaños. Éramos dos. We ate in a restaurant to celebrate my birthday. There were two of us.

Worked example

Describe a meal out to celebrate your sister's engagement.

El año pasado comí en un restaurante para celebrar el compromiso de mi hermana. Comimos y bebimos muchas cosas.

AIMING HIGHER

Anoche fui a cenar con mi familia a un restaurante muy popular. Cenamos comida china y estaba deliciosa. De primer plato, comimos un arroz con verduras, y después unas costillas riquísimas. Creo que iré con mis amigos la semana que viene. ¡Será guay!

Using different forms of **comer** and **beber** in the preterite shows **good knowledge of verbs**. Use a dictionary for words you don't know and to find more interesting vocabulary, e.g. **el compromiso** – engagement.

- Using **creo que** (I think that) adds **more detail** and works in a different opinion expression.
- The use of a third tense (in the future forms **iré** and **será**) shows you can deal with **more complex** grammar.

Now try this

Describe a meal out that you have had, in 100 words.

Try to include:
- why you went
- what you ate and drank
- what the food was like
- whether you will go back to the restaurant or not.

Opinions about food

Make sure you can say what kind of food you really like – and what you hate!

Opiniones sobre la comida

¿Qué tipo de comida te gusta?	What kind of food do you like?
Mi comida favorita es …	My favourite food is …
la comida española	Spanish food
la comida china	Chinese food
la comida griega	Greek food
la comida india	Indian food
la comida italiana	Italian food
porque es …	because it's …
delicioso/a	delicious
graso/a	fatty
malo/a para la salud	unhealthy
nutritivo/a	nutritious
picante	spicy
rico/a	tasty
sabroso/a	tasty
salado/a	salty
sano/a	healthy

Using -ísimo for emphasis

Add -ísimo to the end of an adjective to make it stronger.

buenísimo	really good
riquísimo	really tasty

Expressing a range of opinions

Creo que …	I think that …
♥ Me gusta …	I like …
✗ No me gusta (nada) …	I don't like … (at all).
✗ Odio …	I hate …
En mi opinión …	In my opinion …

Creo que la comida española es buenísima.
I think Spanish food is really nice.

Odio las anchoas porque son saladas.
I hate anchovies because they are salty.

Don't forget to make adjectives agree!

Worked example   LISTENING 29   target B

Listen and put a cross in the correct box.
In her restaurant María cooks:
Spanish food. ☒
Chinese food. ☐
English food. ☐

– ¡Hola! Me llamo María. Soy cocinera y trabajo en un restaurante español de Londres.

Listening strategies

- Be patient and continue to listen CAREFULLY even if the answers don't come up in the first few sentences.
- Remember that people don't always describe things directly. Listen out for COMPARATIVES and use these to work out opinions which aren't stated directly.

Now try this   LISTENING 30   target B

Listen to the whole recording and put a cross by the correct endings.

1 María thinks Spanish food is: healthy. ☐   fatty. ☐   typical. ☐

2 María doesn't cook at home because:
she doesn't have time. ☐   her boyfriend is Greek. ☐   she eats at the restaurant. ☐

3 María thinks Greek food is: horrible. ☐   quite good. ☐   really tasty. ☐

Restaurant problems

Learn these expressions to help you deal with problems in a restaurant.

Problemas en un restaurante

Falta un cuchillo.	I need a knife.
Está demasiado salado.	It's too salty.
El vino está malo.	The wine is bad.
No hay sal.	There's no salt.
El café está frío.	The coffee is cold.
Sabe mal.	It tastes awful.

Hay un error en la cuenta.
There's an error in the bill.

Llevo media hora esperando.
I've been waiting for half an hour!

El tenedor / El plato está sucio.
The fork / The plate is dirty.

No hay ni aceite ni vinagre.
There's no oil or vinegar.

No está bien hecho.
It's not cooked through.

Los camareros son lentos y antipáticos.
The waiters are slow and unfriendly.

No pedí este plato.
I didn't order this dish.

Using the verb faltar

Some Spanish verbs are only used in the THIRD PERSON singular and plural. Faltar is the verb to use if something is missing or needed. You use the plural form when you need more than one thing.

Falta una cuchara.
I need a spoon.

Faltan un cuchillo
y un tenedor.
I need a knife and fork.

Phrases you may hear In a listening task include:

Lo siento, le traigo otro.
I'm sorry, I'll bring you another.

¿Quiere un postre gratis?
Would you like a free dessert?

¿Quiere un reembolso?
Would you like a refund?

Worked example

Read the text.

Cenamos en su restaurante anoche y tuvimos muchos problemas. Habíamos reservado una mesa para las ocho y veinte pero estuvimos esperando media hora en el bar. Mi mujer pidió el bistec pero estaba poco hecho, y el camarero nos trajo vino tinto en vez del vino blanco que pedimos. Quisimos un postre pero el camarero nunca llegó así que pedí la cuenta. Además, el camarero perdió mi abrigo y tuvimos que salir porque mi mujer estaba enferma.
Juan Vázquez

Which of these sentences is correct?

They booked a table for 8.20. ☒

They had to wait in the bar for an hour. ☐

Now try this

Read the text again and put a cross by the other **three** correct sentences.

A The steak was undercooked. ☐

B They didn't order dessert. ☐

C The waiter brought them red wine. ☐

D The waiter made a mistake with the bill. ☐

E At the end of the evening something was lost. ☐

F At the end of the evening Señor Vázquez didn't feel well. ☐

Shops

Make sure you learn the names of shops for your listening and reading exams.

Las tiendas

un estanco	a tobacconist
un supermercado	a supermarket
una carnicería	a butcher's
una droguería	a shop selling household goods
una joyería	a jeweller's
una papelería	a stationer's
una peluquería	a hairdresser's
una tienda de muebles	a furniture shop
una tienda de ultramarinos	a grocer's
unos grandes almacenes	a department store

Cognates

- Look out for cognates in Spanish. These are words that RESEMBLE, or are the SAME AS, words in English, e.g. farmacia – pharmacy, quiosco – (newspaper) kiosk, rugby.

- Look out for ways to CONNECT Spanish words too. This will help you work out the meaning of new words and help you remember vocabulary, e.g.

flor – flower – floristería – florist's

libro – book – librería – bookshop

pan – bread – panadería – bakery

una pastelería

una tienda de ropa

Librería is a bookshop, not a library.

Worked example

READING   **target E**

Read this sign in a department store and answer the questions.

El Corte Español
Salamanca

Directorio
6 Cafetería. Restaurante. Terraza.
5 Peluquería. Muebles y Decoración.
4 Joyería. Discos. Estanco.
3 Moda Hombre y Mujer
2 Juguetes y Videojuegos
1 Floristería. Librería.

What floor would you visit to buy video games? 2

- Once you've decided on an answer, **cross out** the relevant word in the text, so you don't waste time considering it again.
- **Check** your answers when you've finished, to make sure you're happy with your choices.

Reading strategies

- Look for cognates – use what you know in English AND Spanish (e.g. you might not know juguetes, but you do know jugar – play)
- Use your head! Think about what is likely to appear on a shop sign.

Now try this

READING   **target E**

Read the sign again and answer these questions.

Which floor would you visit to …

1 have a haircut?
2 buy a man's jumper?
3 buy a watch?
4 buy a dictionary?

Shopping for food

You will need to know words for quantities when you're shopping for food in Spain.

Comprar comida

¿Qué desea?	What would you like?
Deme ..., por favor.	Give me ..., please.
¿Algo más?	Anything else?
Nada más.	Nothing else.
el jamón	ham
el pan	bread
el pato	duck
el pescado	fish
el queso	cheese
el salchichón	salami-type sausage
la carne de cordero	lamb
la harina	flour
la leche	milk
la leche entera	full-cream milk
la mermelada	jam
la miel	honey
la ternera	veal
las galletas	biscuits
las sardinas	sardines
los huevos	eggs

Quantities

In Spanish you use de (of) with quantities, even with grams and kilograms:

una lata de tomates	a tin of tomatoes
una barra de pan	a loaf of bread
una caja de galletas	a box of biscuits
una botella de agua	a bottle of water
un cartón de leche	a carton of milk
un paquete de caramelos	a bag of sweets
doscientos cincuenta gramos de ...	250 grams of ...
quinientos gramos de ...	500 grams of ...
medio kilo de ...	half a kilo of...
un kilo de ...	I kilo of ...
una docena de huevos	a dozen eggs

Worked example

READING · target C

Read the text.

FIESTA DE LA TORTILLA

El domingo en la plaza de la Iglesia tuvo lugar la fiesta de la tortilla organizada por el ayuntamiento. Paco Pastrana hizo la mejor tortilla y por eso recibió quinientos euros. Paco dijo que su tortilla tenía huevos, patatas, cebolla y también champiñones. Por la noche todos pudieron sentarse en la plaza, comer tortilla gratis y comprar vino.

Read and put a cross by the correct ending.

The competition was on:

Saturday. ☐   Sunday. ☒   Monday. ☐

You might not know what **el ayuntamiento** means but you can use what you **do** know to work out the answer.

Look at the options: you probably know 'church' – iglesia – and 'tourist office' – oficina de turismo – so you can rule those out. That leaves the town hall – the correct answer!

Now try this

READING · target C

Read the text again and put a cross by the correct endings.

1 The competition was organised by: the church. ☐   the town hall. ☐   the tourist office. ☐
2 The winner received: fifteen euros. ☐   fifty euros. ☐   five hundred euros. ☐
3 The extra ingredient in Paco's tortilla was: mushrooms. ☐   ham. ☐   cheese. ☐

At the market

Make sure you know a wide range of words for food. It will help you make your answers more varied and interesting.

En el mercado

un melocotón	a peach
un plátano	a banana
una ciruela	a plum
unas frambuesas	raspberries
una naranja	an orange
unas uvas	grapes
un pepino	cucumber
una col	cabbage
una coliflor	cauliflower
unas judías	beans
unas judías verdes	green beans
una lechuga	lettuce

unas cerezas   una manzana

unas fresas

una piña

Some or any?

The plural form of the indefinite article means 'some' or 'any'.

(masculine) unos plátanos

(feminine) unas manzanas

una cebolla   unos champiñones   unos guisantes   unas patatas   unas zanahorias

Worked example

READING   target G

What is on the shopping list? Put a cross in **four** correct boxes.

- Unos tomates
- Unas frambuesas
- Unas cebollas
- Unas zanahorias
- Unos guisantes
- Unos plátanos
- Unas cerezas
- Unas ciruelas

A ☐   B ☒   C ☐
D ☐   E ☐   F ☐
G ☐   H ☐   I ☐
J ☐

EXAM ALERT!

Make sure you only put the number of crosses you are asked for – never more. If you're not sure, have a guess.

Some students don't do as well as they should in these picture tasks because they do not recognise basic vocabulary. Learn food vocabulary carefully to give yourself the best chance.

This was a real exam question that a lot of students struggled with – **be prepared!**

ResultsPlus

Now try this

READING   target G

Read the text again and complete the activity by putting a cross in **three** more boxes.

Signs in shops

Learn these common signs so that you can find your way around Spanish shops.

Letreros de las tiendas

las rebajas	sales
reducido	reduced
un descuento del cincuenta por ciento	50% discount
una oferta especial / una oferta de ocasión	a special offer
liquidación de invierno	winter clearance sales
los mejores precios	the best prices
las horas de apertura	opening hours
abierto	open
cerrado	closed
el escaparate	shop window
una reducción	a reduction
la bolsa de la compra	shopping bag
la cesta	basket
el carrito de la compra	trolley
la caja	till
salida	exit
ascensores	lifts
agotado	sold out

Time expressions

Time expressions also appear frequently on signs.

mañana	morning
por la mañana	in the morning
tarde	afternoon
por la tarde	in the afternoon
hoy	today
mañana	tomorrow
a partir de	from
ahora	now
desde	since / from
después / luego	then

Seasons

primavera   verano   otoño   invierno

Worked example 🎧 31 target C

Listen and put a cross by the **four** correct sentences.

A The sale goods are low quality. ☐
B The sale goods are at low prices. ☒
C The shop is open 10 hours a day. ☐
D The shop is open all week. ☐
E There's a sale on because it's spring. ☐
F The 50% discount is available today. ☐
G There is a bigger discount if you spend over 70€. ☐
H The biggest discount available is more than 50%. ☐

– ¡No te pierdas esta oportunidad! Todo lo que necesitas a la mejor calidad y a precio de liquidación.

Listening strategies

• Remember to read the questions BEFORE you listen: this will help you focus on the right information. In E, for example, you're listening out for the word for 'spring'. Try to recall the seasons vocabulary before you listen, so that you know what to listen out for.

• Sometimes you need to make DEDUCTIONS when you listen. You might not be told explicitly whether the shop is open all week. But you can use the information that is given – the days the shop will be OPEN – to work out the correct answer.

Now try this 🎧 32 target C

Listen to the whole recording and complete the activity by finding the other **three** correct sentences.

Clothes and colours

You can talk about clothes in different contexts, so be ready to use a variety of tenses.

La ropa y los colores

la ropa informal	casual clothes
la ropa elegante	smart clothes
un cinturón	a belt
un jersey	a jumper
un sombrero	a hat
un traje	a suit
un traje de baño	a swimming costume
un vestido	a dress
una camisa	a shirt
una camiseta	a T-shirt
una chaqueta	a jacket
una falda	a skirt
unas botas	boots
unas zapatillas de deporte	trainers
unos pantalones	trousers
unos vaqueros	jeans
unos zapatos	shoes
de cuadros	checked
de rayas	striped

Using a variety of tenses

You can:

* say what you NORMALLY wear (present).
  Llevo una blusa.   I wear a blouse.
* say what you wore ON ONE OCCASION (preterite).
  Llevé una falda.   I wore a skirt.
* say what you USED TO wear (imperfect).
  Llevaba una corbata.   I used to wear a tie.
* say what you WILL wear (future).
  Llevaré un cinturón.   I will wear a belt.

Colours

verde   negro
amarillo   rosa
rojo   marrón
blanco   azul

Make sure the colour words **agree** and are placed **after** the item of clothing, e.g.

una falda negra
a black skirt

Worked example

Write about what you wore for a special occasion.

AIMING HIGHER
Normalmente llevo ropa informal, como jerseys porque es más cómoda y cuesta menos, pero para la boda de mi hermana llevé un vestido azul que era muy bonito y los zapatos de racon altos. Todo el mundo me halagaba. Este fin de semana llevaré mi vestido nuevo para la fiesta de mi amigo y estaré guapa pero no voy a calzar los mismos zapatos porque me hacen daño. Todo el mundo va estar celoso de mí.

Aiming higher

* Use verbs in a VARIETY of tenses:
  Normalmente llevo ... Para la boda llevé ... Este fin de semana llevaré.
* Express an OPINION in a past tense. Why not try using the imperfect? e.g. Me encantaba llevar ... (I used to love wearing ...)
* Aim even higher by using INTERESTING VERBS such as halagar (to flatter) – especially impressive in the imperfect – and expressions like celoso de mí (jealous of me).

Now try this

Write 60 words about what you wore on a special occasion.

Improve your answer by including an opinion using a **past tense**.
Check that all your adjectives **agree**.

Shopping for clothes

If you're talking about clothes shopping, be ready to ASK as well as to answer questions.

Comprar ropa

Me gustaría comprar estas botas negras.	I would like to buy those black boots.
¿Quiere probárselo?	Would you like to try it on?
¿Me las puedo probar?	Can I try them on?
¿Qué número / talla usa usted?	What size are you?
¿Qué tal le queda(n)?	How do(es) it / they fit?
No los / las tengo.	We don't have them.
No lo / la tenemos en este tamaño.	We don't have them in this size.
Me los / las llevo.	I'll take them.
los probadores	the changing rooms
esta chaqueta	this jacket
estos vaqueros	these jeans
Mi número de zapato es el 39.	My shoe size is 39.
Busco un vestido, talla 38.	I am looking for a dress in size 38.

Remember: use **talla** for clothes and **número** for shoes.

Using the verb quedar

Use the verb quedar to talk about how clothes fit you or suit you: queda for a SINGLE item and quedan for MORE THAN ONE.

La falda me queda bien.	The skirt suits me.
Las botas me quedan mal.	The boots don't fit me.

Direct object pronouns

	Masculine	Feminine
it	lo	la
them	los	las

– Estos zapatos son demasiado pequeños.
– Lo siento, no los tengo en su número.

Worked example

LISTENING 33 | target C

Listen, who said this?

This size is too small for me. María

María – Hola. Me gustaría probarme esta falda roja pero esta talla me queda pequeña.

Listening strategies

- Remember to read the questions BEFORE you listen and anticipate key words to listen out for.
- Key words to listen out for here are: clothes, sizes and colours
- Don't forget to listen carefully for PRONOUNS, too!

Now try this

LISTENING 34 | target C

Listen and write who said these sentences: María, Juan or Ana.

1 They suit me. ....
2 These are too big for me. ....
3 Can I try them on? ....
4 Yellow doesn't suit me. ....
5 I'll take them. ....

Returning items

Use this vocabulary to help you return problem items and refer to them accurately using demonstrative adjectives.

Devolver artículos

Quiero cambiar este / esta ...	I want to change this ...
Quiero quejarme.	I want to complain.
Está estropeado.	It's broken.
Es demasiado grande.	It's too big.
Me están demasiado pequeños.	They're too small for me.
Está roto.	It's broken.
Está rasgado.	It's ripped.
Le falta un botón.	A button is missing.
No le gusta a mi madre.	My mother doesn't like it.
Hay un agujero / una mancha.	There is a hole / a stain.
No funciona.	It doesn't work.
Tengo el recibo.	I have the receipt.
Quiero un reembolso.	I want a refund.
Quiero hablar con el director.	I want to speak to the manager.
Me parece inaceptable.	That's unacceptable.

Demonstrative adjectives

> Grammar page 85

Demonstrative adjectives (this, that, these, those) are used with a noun and must agree with that noun.

		masculine	feminine
this / these			
singular		este	esta
plural		estos	estas
that / those			
singular		ese	esa
plural		esos	esas

este reloj — this watch
esta camiseta — this T-shirt

estas botas — these boots
estos zapatos — those shoes

Worked example 🎧 35 target B

Listen and put a cross next to the **four** correct sentences.

A The man bought the jacket last week. ☒
B There's a button missing on the jacket. ☐
C He discovered the fault today. ☐
D He wants to get his money back. ☐
E He wants another jacket. ☐
F He doesn't need his receipt. ☐
G The man doesn't have his receipt any more. ☐
H He's going to return the next day. ☐

```
Compré esta chaqueta la
semana pasada en su tienda.
```

You might not know **un agujero** (a hole) but if you don't hear the word **falta** when the man describes the problem, you know that you can rule out sentence B as a correct option.

EXAM ALERT!

Don't cross more than the number of boxes asked for! Read the instruction carefully to avoid making careless mistakes.

```
This was a real exam
question that a lot
of students struggled
with - be prepared!
```
ResultsPlus

Now try this 🎧 36 target B

Listen to the whole recording and complete the activity by finding the other **three** correct sentences.

Online shopping

Shopping on the internet has its own vocabulary that you need to learn.

Hacer compras por Internet

las ventajas	the advantages
las desventajas	the disadvantages
comprar	to buy
los precios	the prices
ahorrar tiempo	to save time
desplazarse	to travel
evitar colas	to avoid queues
encontrar	to find
una mayor cantidad	a greater quantity
una variedad	a variety
bajo / caro / barato	low / expensive / cheap
rápido / fácil	quick / easy
una tarjeta de crédito	a credit card
los pagos	the payments / costs
la devolución	the return
el fraude	fraud
los artículos	ítems
estar abierto	to be open
las 24 horas del día	24 hours a day
los 365 días del año	365 days a year

So, so much, so many

tan + adjective = so
tan caro   so expensive

tanto + noun =   so much
tanto tiempo   so much time

tantos + noun =   so many
tantos artículos   so many items

Hace tanto calor en verano.
It's so hot in summer.

Hay tantos ingleses que viven en España.
There are so many English people living in Spain.

Es tan rápido hoy en día viajar en tren. It's so quick to go by train nowadays.

Worked example   READING   target A

Read the text.

Las ventajas de comprar por Internet son claras: se evita hacer colas y también con sólo hacer clic se pueden comprar artículos que no se encuentran en tu país. Pero comprar por Internet también tiene sus desventajas. Algunas de ellas son los pagos, la devolución de los artículos y el ser víctima de fraude. Pese a todo esto, es posible que en un futuro no muy lejano la mayoría de nuestras compras se hagan de esta forma. Lo importante es que los consumidores tengan tanto cuidado en el mundo virtual como el mundo real.

Answer the question in English.

Mention **two** advantages of buying online.
avoiding queues / finding items not in your country

Recognising the cognate **fraude** would give you one of the disadvantages. Using **logic** and general **background knowledge** of the topic would help you work out the others.

Now try this   READING   target A

Read the text again and answer these questions in English.

1 Mention two disadvantages of buying online.
2 What does the text suggest might happen in the future?
3 What is it important for consumers to do?

Shopping opinions

Use the language here to help you give your opinion about shopping.

Opiniones sobre ir de compras

¿Te gusta ir de compras?	Do you like shopping?
Odio ir de compras.	I hate shopping.
los centros comerciales	shopping centres
las tiendas	shops
el dinero	money
ir a la moda	to be fashionable
los grandes almacenes	department stores
ir de compras	to shop
hacer cola	to queue
comprar	to buy
vender	to sell
el escaparate/la vitrina	the shop window
gastar dinero	to spend money
el envase	packaging

Try to work in different tenses:
Fui de compras.	I went shopping.
Compré ...	I bought ...
Compraré ...	I will buy ...
Volveré ...	I will return ...

Negatives
Grammar page 98

no goes before the verb:

No voy.	I don't go.

Other negatives go either side of the verb, forming a sandwich:

nada	nothing, not at all
No tengo nada.	I have nothing (at all).
nadie	nobody
No hay nadie aquí.	There's nobody here.
nunca / jamás	never
No voy nunca a Londres.	I never go to London.
ni... ni...	neither... nor...
No me gusta ni el azul ni el verde.	I don't like blue or green.

No me gusta nada ir de compras.
I don't like shopping at all.

Worked example

🔊 SPEAKING

¿Te gusta ir de compras?

Odio ir de compras. No me interesa nada la moda. Hay siempre demasiada gente y todos los jóvenes llevan las mismas marcas. Cuando tengo que comprar ropa, utilizo Internet. Es más fácil.

AIMING HIGHER Me encanta ir de compras, sobre todo para ver los escaparates de las tiendas de marca. Son impresionantes. Ayer fui a Manchester porque en mi pueblo no hay ninguna tienda de moda. Me lo pasé bien y gasté mucho dinero. Volveré la semana que viene porque vi un vestido precioso que creo que me voy a comprar.

Aiming higher

- EXTEND your answer by giving your opinion about a past shopping trip. The use of a preterite tense verb (fui) and a negative phrase (ninguna tienda) in the second answer adds variety.

- In the second answer, the use of the FUTURE tense (volveré, compraré) to say that she will return to Manchester and she will buy a new dress adds another tense.

Now try this

🔊 SPEAKING

Answer this question. Speak for about 30 seconds.
- ¿Te gusta ir de compras?

You could mention:
- a recent trip and what you bought
- what you will buy in the future.

Travelling

On this page you will find ways to help you understand and talk about travel problems.

Viajar

Hay un retraso ... There is a delay ...
  debido a una huelga de   due to an
  los controladores aéreos   air traffic controllers' strike

  debido a la niebla   due to fog
  por obras   due to repairs
Estoy enfadado/a. I'm angry.
Les informamos que ... We inform you that ...
los pasajeros passengers
El vuelo está retrasado.
The flight is delayed.
El tren está anulado / cancelado.
The train is cancelled.
Se han perdido mis maletas.
My suitcases have been lost.
La máquina no funciona.
The machine does not work.
He perdido mi tarjeta de embarque.
I've lost my boarding card.
La cola para facturar es demasiado larga.
The check-in queue is too long.

How to say 'because of'

In Spanish, there are several ways to describe what has caused an event or situation:

- a causa de   because of
  A causa de una huelga en Francia no hay vuelos a Paris.
  Because of a strike in France there are no flights to Paris.

- debido a   due to
  Debido a una tormenta en Nueva York, el vuelo IB6789 está retrasado.
  Due to a storm in New York the flight IB6789 is delayed.

- gracias a   thanks to
  Gracias a Iberia, llegaré a tiempo.
  Thanks to Iberia, I will arrive on time.

Worked example · LISTENING 37 · target A

You are waiting for a flight and hear this announcement.
Listen and underline the correct option.
The flight is boarding / cancelled / <u>delayed</u>.

- The word **debido** alerts you to the fact that it's a problem, so not an announcement about boarding.
- Even if you don't know the key word **retraso** (delay), the inclusion of a time – **treinta minutos** – also helps you work out it's a delay and not a cancellation.

– Atención, por favor, todos los pasajeros del vuelo número IB 6639 con destino a Málaga. Les informamos que hay un retraso de treinta minutos debido a la niebla.

Now try this · LISTENING 38 · target A

Listen to the rest of the recording and underline the correct options.
1 The announcement is about flight **4657 / 4765 / 4567**.
2 The flight is **boarding / cancelled / delayed**.
3 The problem is due to **bad weather / a strike / a late plane**.

Remember that you may not hear the words **exactly** as they are in the question. Be prepared to listen out for a **range** of possible vocabulary.

Travel problems

This page helps you to describe problems encountered at a train station and to use the pluperfect when relating past events.

Problemas durante un viaje

coger un tren	to catch a train
perder el tren	to miss the train
un billete de ida y vuelta	a return ticket
tarde / temprano	late / early
el viaje	the journey
durar	to last
llegar	to arrive
salir	to leave
esperar	to wait
parar	to stop
funcionar	to work
los servicios	the toilets
los asientos	the seats
sucio / limpio	dirty / clean
cambiar	to change
directo	direct
ya	already

The pluperfect tense

The pluperfect tense describes what someone HAD DONE or something that HAD HAPPENED.

	haber in the imperfect +	past participle
yo	había	salido
tú	habías	llegado
él / ella	había	esperado

Cuando mi madre llegó, el tren había salido ya.
When my mother arrived, the train had already left.

Worked example · READING · target B

Read the text.

La última vez que cogí el tren fue un desastre. Llegué a la estación tarde y el tren había salido ya. Tuve que comprar un nuevo billete porque había dejado el mío en casa. Cuando subí al tren tuve que ir de pie durante el viaje porque no había reservado un asiento. Además, los servicios no funcionaban y estaban cerrados y el tren estaba sucio.

Don't be put off by seeing a variety of **tenses** – here, the preterite and pluperfect. Just focus on the **language** to answer the questions.

Put a cross next to the **four** correct sentences.

1 His first train trip did not go well. ☒
2 He arrived at the station early. ☐
3 He missed his train. ☐
4 He already had a ticket that he was able to use. ☐
5 Someone was sitting in his seat. ☐
6 He had to stand for the whole journey. ☐
7 The train broke down. ☐
8 The train wasn't clean. ☐

Now try this · READING · target B

Read the text again and complete the activity by finding the other **three** correct sentences.

Money problems

Use this page to revise money vocabulary and to practise using the imperfect continuous.

Problemas con el dinero

la oficina de correos	post office
el banco	bank
¿Qué pasó?	What happened?
¿Qué ha pasado?	What has happened?
hacer una denuncia	to report a crime
agarrarse	to grab
el ladrón	the thief
una declaración	a statement
caerse	to fall
la acera	the pavement
tropezar	to bump into

He perdido mi tarjeta de crédito.
I have lost my credit card.

cuando iba viajando en el tren
when I was travelling on the train

Alguien ha robado mi monedero / mi cartera.
Someone has stolen my wallet.

cuando estaba comprando recuerdos
when I was buying souvenirs

The imperfect continuous tense

Grammar page 92

The imperfect continuous tense describes something that WAS HAPPENING at a certain moment in the past. It is formed using the appropriate part of estar in the imperfect tense, and the gerund.

Estaba caminando por la ciudad.
I was walking around the city.

Estaba cruzando la calle.
He was crossing the street.

Estaba sacando dinero del cajero automático.
I was taking money out of the cash machine.

Worked example

LISTENING 39   target A*

Claudia is at the police station reporting a robbery. Listen and answer the question in English.

When did the robbery happen?

the day before yesterday

– Pues mire, anteayer fui al centro de la ciudad y estaba sacando dinero del cajero automático cuando un ladrón me agarró el bolso.

EXAM ALERT!

- In the 2011 exam, some candidates confused **anteayer** with **ayer**. Remember to listen really carefully to catch small details.
- A few candidates answered in Spanish – and got no marks. Remember to read the instructions carefully and always answer in the same language as the question.

This was a real exam question that a lot of students struggled with – **be prepared!**   ResultsPlus

Now try this

LISTENING 40   target A*

Listen to the whole recording and answer these questions in English.

1 What was Claudia doing in town?
2 What happened to Claudia when she tried to chase the thief? Give **two** details.
3 How did she describe the thief? Give **two** details.
4 Apart from money, what exactly did she have in her bag?
5 Why does she feel particularly sad about her loss?

Lost property and theft

Use this language to cope with problems when you lose a possession or have it stolen.

En la oficina de objetes perdidos

la oficina de objetos perdidos	lost property office
He perdido ...	I've lost...
¿Dónde y cuándo?	Where and when?
en la sala de espera	in the waiting room
en los probadores	in the changing rooms
¿Cómo es?	What's it like?
Es de oro / plata.	It's gold / silver.
caro / barato	expensive / cheap
nuevo / viejo	new / old

Possessive pronouns

> Grammar page 83

Possessive pronouns are used to indicate the owner of an item. They agree with the object, NOT with the person.

Estos pendientes son míos.
These earrings are mine.

Este collar es tuyo.
That necklace is yours.

un abrigo   un anillo   un bolso   unos pendientes   un ordenador portátil   un sombrero   una cartera / un monedero

una maleta   un paraguas   unas gafas de sol   unas llaves   una pulsera a bracelet   un collar a necklace

Worked example

> LISTENING 41   target C

Listen and complete the grid.

Item	bracelet
Description (2 details)	
Where exactly	
When	

- Buenos días, he perdido una pulsera.

Listening strategies

- The answers will be in the SAME ORDER as the questions. You can use this to help you find the information you need.
- If you miss an answer keep listening and try to answer the other questions. You will get a second chance.

EXAM ALERT!

Some students waste the time they have before they listen and so are not well prepared. Always read questions before you listen so you know what **type** of language you're listening for.

Students have struggled with exam questions similar to this – **be prepared!**

ResultsPlus

Now try this

> LISTENING 42   target C

Listen to the whole recording and complete the activity.

Complaints and problems

Mentioning a problem in your presentation will allow you to use more complex language.

Quejas y problemas

una avería	a breakdown
el carnet de identidad	ID card
la tarjeta de crédito	credit card
un robo	a theft
un ladrón	a thief
el seguro	insurance
estar enfermo	to be ill
la comisaría	the police station
la verdad	the truth
asegurar	to insure
desaparecer	to disappear
dejar	to leave behind
preocuparse	to worry
caer	to fall
tener mala suerte	to have bad luck
anular	to cancel
chocar	to crash
atropellar	to knock down
quejarse	to complain
dañar	to damage

Irregular past participles

Grammar page 95

Infinitive		Past participle	
abrir	to open	abierto	opened
decir	to say	dicho	said
escribir	to write	escrito	written
hacer	to do	hecho	done
poner	to put	puesto	put
romper	to break	roto	broken
ver	to see	visto	seen
volver	to return	vuelto	returned

He roto mi cámara.
I have broken my camera.

Worked example

LISTENING 43 · target C

Listen and put a cross in the correct boxes.
Who …

A spent too much money?
B will go and see a doctor?
C doesn't like English food?
D broke their leg?
E lost their ID card?

	A	B	C	D	E
Mr Sánchez					
Mrs Sánchez	x				
Julia					
Martín					
Jaime					

– Creo que Londres es una ciudad preciosa. Inglaterra es un país barato para nosotros pero he gastado demasiado dinero estas vacaciones.

- Listen out for **cognates** to help you (identidad) and be prepared to work out information when the language you are listening for isn't explicitly used. You don't hear 'Mr Sánchez' but **mi marido**.

- Listen carefully for **small words**, especially in compound tenses. You know Mrs Sánchez is talking, as it is a female voice, and when she says **he gastado**, you need to be able to remember that this is the 'I' form of the verb.

Now try this

LISTENING 44 · target C

Listen to the whole recording and complete the activity.

School subjects

You need to be able to say what subjects you study, what you think of them and why.

Las asignaturas

Estudio ... I study ...

el teatro   el francés   la geografía   la música

la tecnología   el inglés   la educación física   la historia

la informática   el dibujo   las matemáticas   las ciencias

Giving opinions

Grammar page 99

- me gusta (I like) literally translates as 'it pleases me'.
- If the subject is plural, use me gustan.
- me encanta (I love) and me interesa (I'm interested in) work in the same way.

Me gusta la química.	I like chemistry.
Me encanta el español.	I love Spanish.
Me interesan las ciencias.	I'm interested in science.

Other ways to give your opinion:

Odio / Detesto	I hate
Encuentro	I find
Creo / Pienso	I think
Es / Son ...	It's / They're ...

interesante / fácil / útil / práctico
interesting / easy / useful / practical

difíciles / aburridos / inútiles / complicados
difficult / boring / useless / complicated

Worked example 🎧 45 target D

Listen and put a cross in **one** correct box.
1 Marcela enjoys studying languages. ☒
2 She thinks English is more useful than French. ☐

— Buenos días, señor director. Soy Marcela.
— Hola, Marcela, ¿qué te gustaría estudiar en enero?
— Me gustan mucho el inglés y el francés. Es muy útil estudiar idiomas.

Look out for other **links**: here, the **inglés / francés** link to languages is a useful one to spot.

EXAM ALERT!

Students frequently failed to link **química** or **física** with science, and so failed to see that sentence 3 was correct. Good vocabulary knowledge is essential for the listening exam.

This was a real exam question that a lot of students struggled with – **be prepared!**

ResultsPlus

Now try this 🎧 46 target D

Listen to the whole recording and write the correct names (Marcela or Francisco) to answer the questions.
1 Who thinks art is a waste of time?
2 Who likes science?
3 Who finds IT difficult?
4 Who hates PE?

School description

You can use this page to talk about the facilities at your school.

Mi colegio

Mi colegio es grande / pequeño / moderno.	My school is big / small / modern.
(No) hay ...	There is(n't) ...
(No) tenemos ...	We (don't) have ...
unos laboratorios	science laboratories
unos vestuarios	changing rooms
unas aulas	classrooms
un gimnasio	a gym
una biblioteca	a library
una sala de profesores	a staffroom
un campo de fútbol	a football pitch
una piscina	a swimming pool
un salón de actos	a hall
un patio	a playground
las instalaciones deportivas	sporting facilities
buenos / malos profesores	good / bad teachers
algunos alumnos traviesos	a few badly-behaved students

Using the verb tener in different tenses

Tener (to have) is a verb you need to know. Be ready to use it in different tenses. It is a radical changing verb (note the vowel change in the present).

	Present	Preterite	Future
I	tengo	tuve	tendré
you	tienes	tuviste	tendrás
he / she / it	tiene	tuvo	tendrá
we	tenemos	tuvimos	tendremos

Remember: you use **tener** to talk about age: Tengo dieciséis años.   I'm 16.

Tenemos un comedor. We have a canteen.

Worked example

Describe your school.

No me gusta mucho mi instituto, es muy viejo y bastante pequeño. No hay biblioteca y hay pocos ordenadores, así que es difícil de hacer los deberes. Construyeron una piscina el año pasado, desafortunadamente no me gusta nada nadar.

This student has done well to include **opinions** as well as introducing the **perfect tense** but he would need to include a greater **variety of vocabulary and tenses** in order to access the higher assessment bands.

AIMING HIGHER Mi instituto es grande y moderno, con muy buenas instalaciones, por eso me gusta mucho. No teníamos muchas instalaciones deportivas así que van a construir una nueva pista de atletismo. Tenemos también aulas nuevas porque se construyeron nuevos edificios el año pasado.

This answer includes more **detail**. Using a passive form like **se construyeron** also shows that you know, and can use, a **wider range** of structures accurately.

Now try this

Describe your school. Write about 100 words
- Say what facilities it has.
- Mention some it doesn't have.
- Include details of how it has changed or will change.

School routine

You may need to be able to describe your school routine as part of your speaking assessment.

La rutina del colegio

Voy al instituto.	I go to school.
Hago mis deberes.	I do my homework.

Llego a las ocho.
I arrive at eight o'clock.

Las clases empiezan a las ocho y media.
Classes start at eight thirty.

Como algo en el recreo.
I have a snack at break.

Charlo con mis amigos.
I chat to my friends.

Las clases terminan a las tres y media.
Classes finish at three thirty.

Después del instituto voy al coro.
After school I go to choir.

Tengo entrenamiento de rugby.
I have rugby training.

Time after time

Time crops up in all sorts of contexts. Keep reviewing it regularly.

Es la una.   Son las nueve.

Son las diez y cuarto.   Son las once y media.

en coche   en autobús   a pie   en bicicleta

Worked example

READING target C

Read the text.

Por la mañana, en invierno, voy al instituto en el coche de los padres de mi amigo pero en verano voy a pie. Llego a las siete y media y las clases terminan a las cuatro todos los días, excepto el miércoles, cuando terminamos a las tres.

Mi prima Paula va andando al instituto pero cuando llueve coge el autobús. Llega a las ocho y media y charla con sus amigos. Las clases terminan a las cuatro. El viernes va a un club de ajedrez. **Manu**

Put a cross by **four** correct sentences.

A In winter Manu goes to school in his parents' car. ☐

B In summer he walks. ☒

C The school day does not always end at the same time. ☐

D Manu arrives at school before eight o'clock. ☐

E Paula always goes to school on foot. ☐

F She sometimes catches the bus. ☐

G She arrives at school at eight. ☐

H She always goes straight home after school. ☐

EXAM ALERT!

Some candidates expect to find in the text an exact Spanish translation of the information they're looking for – but that doesn't happen often. You need to deduce meaning.

This was a real exam question that a lot of students struggled with – be prepared!

ResultsPlus

For sentence D, **las ocho** is the most helpful thing you could find – but it's not in the text. So you need to work out that **a las siete y media** is 'before eight o'clock' – so sentence D is correct.

Now try this

READING target C

Read the text again and put a cross by the other three correct sentences.

Comparing schools

Be prepared to compare Spanish schools with schools in your own country.

Mi colegio, tu colegio

en España …	in Spain …
Hay menos exámenes.	There are fewer exams.
No estudian ciertas asignaturas.	They do not study certain subjects.
Las vacaciones son más largas.	The holidays are longer.
El día escolar es más corto.	The school day is shorter.
Ellos no comen en el instituto.	They don't eat lunch at school.
Los estudiantes llaman a sus profesores por su nombre.	Students call their teachers by their first name.

Los alumnos no tienen que llevar uniforme.
Students do not have to wear uniform.

Aiming higher

Avoid using me gusta and odio all the time – stand out from the crowd by using something more impressive …

No lo aguanto. I can't stand it.	No lo aguantaba. I couldn't stand it.
No lo soporto. I can't bear it.	No lo soportaba. I couldn't bear it.
No me importa. It's not important to me.	No me importaba. It was not important to me
Me enoja. It annoys me.	Me enojaba. It annoyed me.
No es justo. It's not fair.	No era justo. It wasn't fair.
Me da igual. I'm not bothered about …	Me daba igual. I wasn't bothered about …

Worked example

WRITING

Write about the differences between Spanish schools and schools in your country.

Los colegios en España son diferentes que los colegios ingleses. Los alumnos no llevan uniforme y las clases terminan a las dos. Además las vacaciones son más largas: casi tres meses. ¡Me gustaría ir al colegio en España!

AIMING HIGHER En Inglaterra los alumnos llevan uniforme y no lo soporto, pero visité un instituto español durante un intercambio y ¡qué sorpresa! los alumnos españoles no tenían que llevarlo. ¡Qué envidia! ¡No es justo! Lo que más me gusta es que las vacaciones son más largas y por eso preferiría estar en España.

Aiming higher

Try working in expressions like these:

No es justo que …	It's not fair that …
¡Ojalá pudiera tener más vacaciones!	If only I could have more holidays!

- Use of other **tenses** (visité) adds sophistication to this answer.
- **Exclamation phrases** are also useful to show opinions.
- Using more advanced past tense opinions (**No era justo!**) makes your language more complex, as does the inclusion of a conditional **preferiría** (I would prefer).

Now try this

WRITING

Write 100 words about the differences between Spanish schools and schools in your country.

- Work in a range of **opinions** (and use exclamation phrases where appropriate).
- Express a **preference**.

64

At primary school

Use the imperfect tense to talk about what you used to do at primary school.

En la escuela primaria

Cuando tenía diez años era travieso.
When I was 10, I was naughty.

Iba a una escuela de primaria cerca de mi casa.
I used to go to a primary school near my house.

Tenía menos amigos.
I used to have fewer friends.

Jugaba solamente con mis amigas.
I only used to play with my female friends.

Comía los bocadillos que mi madre me preparaba.
I used to eat sandwiches that my mother prepared.

No estudiaba español.   I didn't study Spanish.

Hacía más deporte.
I used to do more sport.

Imperfect tense

Grammar page 92

The imperfect tense is used to describe what USED TO HAPPEN or what WAS HAPPENING.

It is formed as follows:

hablar to speak	comer to eat	vivir to live
hablaba	comía	vivía
hablabas	comías	vivías
hablaba	comía	vivía
hablábamos	comíamos	vivíamos
hablabais	comíais	vivíais
hablaban	comían	vivían

Exam strategies

Learn tenses by chanting them – hablaba, hablabas, hablaba … Start off by reading them, then close your book and see how many you can chant without looking. Keep going until you can do the whole verb.

Worked example

WRITING

Describe your life at primary school.

AIMING HIGHER Cuando tenía diez años era travieso y la escuela primaria era aburrida. Estudiaba más asignaturas y más idiomas. La lengua que más me gustaba era el francés. De pequeño, estaba más contento porque tenía más amigos. La vida era más fácil, no tenía tantos deberes y los profesores eran menos severos.

CONTROLLED ASSESSMENT

Present your work neatly and carefully. Each year, the Examiners' Report states that illegible handwriting loses candidates valuable marks.

Aiming higher

• Including IMPERFECT tense verbs shows a confident and secure use of a tense.

• Use a VARIETY of vocabulary (here, idiomas / lenguas).

• An OPINION phrase in the imperfect (me gustaba) is always a good addition.

Now try this

WRITING

Describe your life at primary school. Write about 100 words.

• Include **opinions** and compare it to life now.
• **Re-read** your work to check for accuracy.
• Check any words you are unsure of in a **dictionary**.

School rules

This page will help you talk about school rules and what you think of them.

Las normas del colegio

en mi instituto …	in my school …
No se puede …	You can't
Está prohibido …	It is forbidden to
No se debe …	You shouldn't …
llevar maquillaje	wear make-up
usar el MP3 en clase	use your MP3 in class
comer chicle	chew gum
usar el móvil	use your mobile
mandar mensajes	send messages
llegar tarde	arrive late
correr por los pasillos	run in the corridors
ser antipático	be unpleasant
hablar mientras que habla el profesor	talk while the teacher is talking

No se puede ser ni desobedientes ni groseros.

You can't be either badly behaved or rude.

Son tontas / necesarias / anticuadas / útiles / inútiles.

They are stupid / necessary / old fashioned / useful / useless.

Key verbs + the infinitive

	querer – want	poder – be able to	deber – should, ought to
I	quiero	puedo	debo
you	quieres	puedes	debes
he / she / it	quiere	puede	debe
we	queremos	podemos	debemos
you	queréis	podéis	debéis
they	quieren	pueden	deben

Quiere llevar pendientes pero no se pueden llevar joyas.
She wants to wear earrings but you can't wear jewellery.

Worked example 🔊 SPEAKING

¿Existen normas en tu instituto?

En mi instituto tengo que llevar uniforme. Odio el uniforme porque es incómodo. En mi opinión, las normas son anticuadas. Son tontas e inútiles pero algunas personas piensan que son necesarias. ¡Qué horror!

AIMING HIGHER

En mi instituto, hay muchas normas. Acaban de introducir una nueva norma y ahora no se permite usar el móvil en clase. ¡Qué horror! Hay que dejarlo en casa, o apagarlo antes de entrar en el instituto. Creo que los profesores son demasiados estrictos.

Use a variety of **opinion** words and **adjectives** (incómodo, anticuados, inútiles) to say not only what you think, but also what others think – this will increase your chance of aiming for a higher grade.

Use **idiomatic phrases** such as **acaban de**. They add variety to your language and make it sound more sophisticated. Try adding an exclamation phrase as well (¡Qué horror!).

Now try this 🔊 SPEAKING

Answer this question. Speak for about one minute.
- ¿Existen normas en tu instituto?

Try to include:
- three opinions/adjectives
- three connectives
- three different phrases with the infinitive
- a Spanish exclamation.

Discussing the future

You can use the ir + infinitive structure to talk about what you are going to do when you finish school.

Que hacer en el futuro

el año que viene/el año próximo	next year
en el futuro	in the future
No estoy seguro.	I'm not sure.
si saco buenas notas ...	if I get good grades ...
Voy a ...	I'm going to ...
estudiar lenguas / idiomas	study languages
ir a la universidad	go to university
buscar un empleo	look for a job
hacer formación	do training
hacer un aprendizaje	do an apprenticeship

seguir estudiando en el instituto
continue studying at school

ir a otro instituto para alumnos de 16 a 18 años
go to a sixth-form college

Near future tense

Grammar page 93

This form of the future is like the English 'going to,' and is used to express plans and intentions.

I	voy		ir
you	vas		buscar
he / she / it	va	a	hacer
we	vamos		seguir
you	vais		trabajar
they	van		estudiar

Voy a ir a la universidad.
I'm going to go to university.

Va a estudiar la música.
He is going to study music.

Worked example

WRITING

What are you going to do after GCSEs?

Voy a estudiar idiomas porque me encanta el español.

Estudiaré ciencias porque me encantan, y voy a ser médico. Es más, saqué buenas notas el año pasado.

AIMING HIGHER Voy a estudiar matemáticas porque me parecen fáciles e interesantes. Creo que es una asignatura muy útil y además es necesaria para poder ir a la universidad a estudiar veterinaria.

Aiming higher

- VARY your tenses – this makes your answer more interesting and lets you show off what you know.
- DEVELOP your answer – always look for opportunities to add more information, e.g. Es más, saqué buenas notas el año pasado.
- Make it STAND OUT – an unusual twist will help distinguish it, e.g. quiero ser traductor de la Unión Europea.
- IMPRESS with interesting structures:
  Mis padres quieren que vaya a la universidad.
  My parents want me to go to university.

Now try this

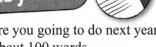
WRITING

What are you going to do next year?
Write about 100 words

Check your own writing against the Edexcel GCSE marking criteria. How well have you done? How can you improve?

Future plans

Using the future tense and the subjunctive to talk about future plans will make your writing and speaking more natural.

Tus planes para el futuro

cuando sea mayor …	when I'm older …
cuando termine la universidad …	when I finish university …
Trabajaré como …	I'll work as …
Trabajaré en el extranjero.	I'll work abroad.
Seré rico.	I'll be rich.
Ganaré la lotería.	I'll win the lottery.
Viajaré mucho.	I'll travel a lot.
Seré famoso.	I'll be famous.
Ganaré mucho dinero.	I'll earn lots of money.
Seré muy feliz.	I will be very happy.

Voy a casarme y tener hijos.
I'm going to get married and have children.

Es un campo en el que me gustaría trabajar.
It's a field in which I would like to work.

Aiming higher

Work out a few expressions using the subjunctive and check them with your teacher.

Subjunctive

Grammar page 97

The subjunctive is used after cuando to talk about an event in the future.

To form the subjunctive, add the following endings to the infinitive:

hablar to speak	comer to eat	vivir to live
hable	coma	viva
hables	comas	vivas
hable	coma	viva
hablemos	comamos	vivamos
habléis	comáis	viváis
hablen	coman	vivan

Cuando tenga veinte años, viajaré mucho.
When I'm 20, I'll travel a lot.

Worked example

SPEAKING

¿Cuáles son tus planes para el futuro?

No sé que voy a hacer después de mis exámenes. Me gustaría trabajar en el extranjero porque me encanta visitar nuevos lugares.

AIMING HIGHER Cuando sea mayor y termine la universidad, viajaré mucho. Ganaré mucho dinero así que seré feliz porque podré comprar mucha ropa.

- Use the future tense (viajaré, ganaré) to say what you **will** do.
- Use connectives (así que, porque) to **justify** your opinions to improve your content grade.
- There is a good example of how to use **cuando** + the subjunctive to add variety to what you say.

Now try this

SPEAKING

Answer this question. Speak for about one minute.
- ¿Cuáles son tus planes para el futuro?

Try to include:
- one or two subjunctive phrases
- two or three future tense phrases
- an opinion phrase.

Jobs

Use this page to help you talk about the different jobs people do.

Empleos

un actor	an actor
un agente de policía / un policía	policeman
un auxiliar de vuelo / una azafata	an airline steward / stewardess
un arquitecto	an architect
un bombero	a firefighter
un camarero	a waiter
un cartero	a postman/woman
un cocinero	a cook
un constructor	builder
un dentista	a dentist
un fontanero	a plumber
un funcionario	a civil servant
un informático	a computer scientist
un ingeniero	an engineer
un médico	a doctor
un panadero	a baker
un periodista	a journalist
un secretario	a secretary
un veterinario	a vet
estar en paro	to be unemployed
el desempleo	unemployment

Using ser to say what jobs people do

Use the verb ser to say what jobs people do. Leave out the indefinite article:

Soy cocinero.   I'm a cook.

Es modelo.   She's a model.

Es camarero.
He's a waiter.

Feminine forms

If the job is done by a woman, change -o to -a:

cocinero ➡ cocinera   camarero ➡ camarera

Note some exceptions:
actor   actriz
These are the same in the masculine and feminine: periodista, dentista

trabajar in different tenses

Present	Imperfect	Future
Trabajo.	Trabajaba.	Trabajaré.
I work.	I used to work.	I will work.

Worked example

🎧 47   target C

Listen and answer the questions in English.

1 How old is Paco? 30
2 Which job did he used to do?
3 Why did he stop doing that job?
4 What does he do now?
5 What job will he do in the future?
6 Why does he want to do this job?

– Hola. Me llamo Paco y tengo treinta años.

Listening strategies

- You'll hear every recording TWICE, so don't worry if you don't catch all the answers on first listening.

- Keep pace with the recording: if you've missed an answer, go on to the next question.

- Don't simply write down the first relevant item of vocabulary you hear. Make sure you listen to the END of a recording before you make your final decision.

Now try this

🎧 48   target C

Listen to the rest of the recording and answer the questions in English.

Job adverts

Job adverts may come up in your reading exam, so learn the vocabulary on this page.

Ofertas de empleo

rellenar un formulario	to fill in a form
un anuncio	an advert
una solicitud	an application
las horas de trabajo	hours of work
una entrevista	an interview
un empleo / un trabajo	a job
una carta	a letter
por hora	per hour
una respuesta / una contestación	an answer
solicitar un empleo	to apply for a job
mandar un fax	to send a fax
con formación	with training
a tiempo parcial	part time
en una empresa	in a company
con un buen sueldo	with a good salary

Prepositions

Prepositions come up in every topic: they give information about WHERE, WHEN and HOW things happen.

a	to / at	entre	between
con	with	para	for/in order to
de	from		
desde	from, since	por	for / by
en	in, on	sin	without
		sobre	on, about

en nuestra página web	on our web page
por fax	by fax
para conocer más informacíon	in order to know more information
sin experiencia	without experience

Worked example

Read the text.

OFERTAS DE EMPLEO

Multimundo – Se necesita secretario sin experiencia para trabajar a tiempo parcial en una empresa multinacional. Interesados deben rellenar una ficha en nuestra página web. Ofrecemos formación, con un buen sueldo y con buenos horarios de trabajo. Las entrevistas tendrán lugar dentro de un mes.

Put a cross in the box by the correct sentence.

The work is not full time. ☒

You need experience to do this job. ☐

Reading strategies

- Answers to questions are usually found in the text in the ORDER in which they are asked – so you won't find the first answer right at the end.
- You need to read carefully to pick up the DETAIL. Reading to get the gist alone will not give you all the information you need.

Now try this

Read the text again and put a cross by **three** further correct sentences.

1 The company has branches in different countries. ☐

2 There is more information on the web page. ☐

3 Training isn't provided. ☐

4 The salary is good. ☐

5 The hours of work are long. ☐

6 The interviews will take place within a month. ☐

CV

You may encounter a CV in a reading exam or writing assessment. If you are creating one, remember to avoid lists and very short sentences.

CV

Nombre y apellido
Paul Jones

Dirección
3 Blake Road, Anytown
AT1 2AZ, Inglaterra

Estado civil   casado

Fecha de nacimiento   13/12/88

Experiencia profesional   camarero

Cualidades personales   dinámico

Aficiones   tenis y fútbol

Idiomas   inglés y español

Correo electrónico   pauljones@ctg.es

Reading strategies

It is easy to work out what the headings in the CV mean by looking at how Paul has filled it in. Using the context to work out the meaning of unknown words is a very useful strategy.

Review **personality adjectives** and the vocabulary for **activities** and **hobbies** in preparation for writing a CV.

Worked example

Read this extract from a CV.

Cualidades personales: simpático, sensible, trabajador, fiable, comprensivo

Cognates are helpful but watch out for **false friends**! Words don't always mean what they seem to. Many students find these three adjectives confusing: **simpático, sensible, comprensivo** Can you use the activity to work out their correct meanings?

Put a cross in the box by the correct ending.
He is:
(a) sympathetic.   ☐
(b) friendly.   ☒
(c) popular.   ☐

Logical thinking!

Remember to think LOGICALLY. Is it likely that someone would use negative adjectives to describe him/herself on a CV? The answer to that may help you rule out some options.

Now try this

Complete the reading activity above by putting a cross in the box by the correct endings.

1 He is:
  (a) sensitive.   ☐
  (b) sensible.   ☐
  (c) sensational.   ☐

2 He:
  (a) is hard to work with.   ☐
  (b) works just as much as he has to.   ☐
  (c) is hardworking.   ☐

3 He:
  (a) is trustworthy.   ☐
  (b) is trusting.   ☐
  (c) is not very strong.   ☐

4 He:
  (a) is understanding.   ☐
  (b) knows everything.   ☐
  (c) is competitive.   ☐

A job application

Use this page to revise job applications vocabulary for your reading or listening exams.

Solicitud de empleo

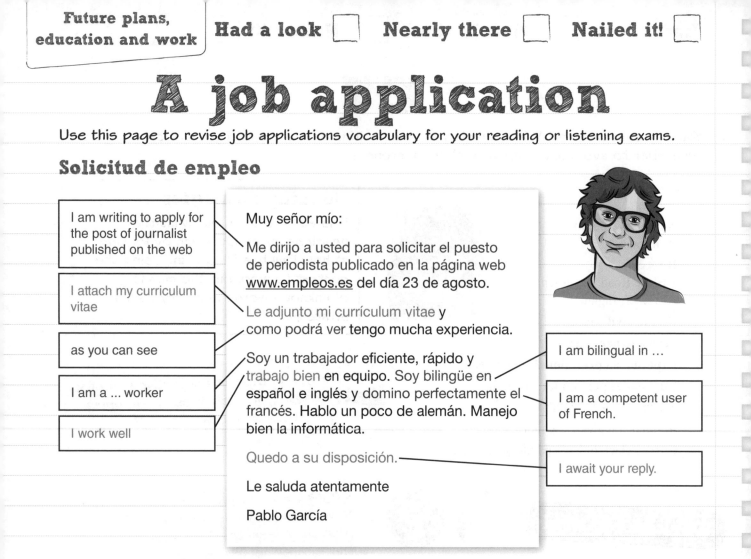

I am writing to apply for the post of journalist published on the web

I attach my curriculum vitae

as you can see

I am a ... worker

I work well

> Muy señor mío:
>
> Me dirijo a usted para solicitar el puesto de periodista publicado en la página web www.empleos.es del día 23 de agosto.
>
> Le adjunto mi currículum vitae y como podrá ver tengo mucha experiencia.
>
> Soy un trabajador eficiente, rápido y trabajo bien en equipo. Soy bilingüe en español e inglés y domino perfectamente el francés. Hablo un poco de alemán. Manejo bien la informática.
>
> Quedo a su disposición.
>
> Le saluda atentamente
>
> Pablo García

I am bilingual in ...

I am a competent user of French.

I await your reply.

Worked example

READING target B

Read the application letter above. Complete these notes.

1 Job applied for: journalist
2 Works well: as part of a team
3 Number of languages spoken: 4

- Make sure you are familiar with the **Edexcel vocabulary list** so that words like **periodista** (journalist) don't catch you out.
- You don't need to answer in full sentences. **Notes** will do.

Now try this

 WRITING

Write a formal letter of application for the job as advertised. Use the example above to help you.

Use the Edexcel GCSE mark scheme to help you aim for the highest grade you can.

> Se buscan dependientes con experiencia. Los horarios de trabajo son fijos y hay que trabajar todos los días, domingos incluidos. Interesados deben mandar una carta por fax para conocer más detalles. Las entrevistas tendrán lugar en nuestras tiendas del centro de la ciudad.

Job interview

As well as revising the vocabulary here, review personality adjectives on page 3.

Una entrevista de empleo

¿Por qué quiere ser ... ?
Why do you want to be ... ?

Quiero ser ... porque me fascina.
I want to be a ... because it fascinates me.

Me encantaría trabajar con ...
I would love to work with ...

¿Qué experiencia tiene?
What experience do you have?

He trabajado como / para ...
I have worked as / for ...

Tengo experiencia en ...
I have experience in ...

He escrito ...
I have written ...

He creado ...
I have created ...

He trabajado en equipo / solo antes.
I have worked in a team / alone before.

¿Qué cualidades tiene?
What qualities do you have?

Soy creativo / simpático / ambicioso.
I am creative / friendly / ambitious.

¿Puede decirme algo más sobre ...?
Can you tell me more about ...?

Perfect tense

Grammar page 95

Remember:

- To form the perfect tense, use:

  haber in the present tense + past participle.

- To form the past participle:

  take off ar / er / ir from the infinitive and add ado / ido / ido.

I	he	
you	has	
he / she / it	ha	hablado
we	hemos	bebido
you	habéis	venido
they	han	

Tenemos que pedir referencias.
We have to ask for references.

Worked example   LISTENING 49   target B

Listen and put a cross by the correct sentence.

Raúl would like to be an air steward.   ☐

He wants to work for a British company.   ☒

— Quiero ser auxiliar de vuelo porque me encanta trabajar con la gente.

EXAM ALERT!

Read the questions before you listen so that you know the type of language and information you are listening out for. You will have five minutes to do this. Don't be distracted by irrelevant detail.

Students have struggled with exam questions similar to this – **be prepared!**   Results Plus

---

Now try this   LISTENING 50   target B

Listen **carefully** for **opinions** – and wait until they are fully expressed rather than jumping to conclusions.

Listen to the whole recording and put a cross by the other **three** correct sentences.

1 He sometimes finds the customers difficult.   ☐
2 He is ambitious.   ☐
3 Belén wants to be a vet.   ☐

4 She has worked with sick people in America.   ☐
5 She has worked in a team.   ☐
6 She is not anti-social.   ☐

Opinions about jobs

Be ready to understand and give a range of opinions on jobs – both positive and negative.

Opiniones sobre empleos 😊

Me gusta tener responsabilidades.	I like having responsibility.
Me encanta trabajar en contacto con la gente.	I love having contact with people.
Me gusta la variedad.	I like variety.
Me encanta trabajar en equipo.	I love working in a team.
Me gusta la flexibilidad.	I like flexibility.
Está bien pagado.	It's well paid.

Opiniones sobre empleos 🙁

Es un trabajo difícil.	It's a difficult job.
Odio trabajar solo.	I hate working alone.
No me gustan los clientes maleducados.	I don't like rude customers.
Está mal pagado.	It's badly paid.
Odio al jefe.	I hate the boss.
Trabajo muchas horas.	I work long hours.
Estoy de pie todo el día.	I'm on my feet all day.

Me gusta ayudar a la gente.
I like helping people.

Es aburrido y monótono.
It's boring and repetitive.

Worked example   READING ①   target B

Read the text.

> Trabajo en una comisaría y me encanta por la responsabilidad que tengo. No gano mucho dinero porque el sueldo es bajo. Trabajo muchas horas, sobre todo los fines de semana, pero la variedad del fin de semana me divierte más. Paco

Put a cross in the box beside the correct ending.

Paco works as a:
postman.   ☐
policeman.   ☒
fireman.   ☐

EXAM ALERT!

Some candidates were distracted by the other options supplied in this question. Often all the options appear somewhere in the text, so you need to read carefully to work out the answers.

> This was a real exam question that a lot of students struggled with – **be prepared!**   ResultsPlus

Knowing the places people work helps you make the link to their job:
una comisaría   a police station.

It is important to learn **little words** like **mucho** (a lot) or **poco** (a little) as they can change the meaning quite radically. In this question, Paco says he does not have much money, so you can rule out 'salary' as the answer to I.

Now try this

Read the text again and complete the activity.

1 Paco likes:
   the hours. ☐   the salary. ☐   the responsibility. ☐

2 Paco:
   works a lot. ☐   doesn't work much. ☐   doesn't work at weekends. ☐

Part-time work

When talking about a part-time job, use tener que to discuss your responsibilities.

Empleos a tiempo parcial

los sábados	on Saturdays
después del colegio	after school
todos los días	every day
Reparto periódicos.	I deliver newspapers.
Hago de canguro.	I babysit.
Trabajo como ...	I work as ...
dependiente	a shop assistant
camarero	a waiter
jardinero	a gardener
Gano mucho / poco.	I earn a lot / little.
Cuido a niños.	I look after children.
Llego a tiempo.	I arrive on time.
Sirvo comida.	I serve food.
Vendo cosas.	I sell things.
Traigo bebidas a los clientes.	I bring drinks to customers.
Es fácil / difícil / interesante / aburrido / variado.	It is easy / difficult / interesting / boring / varied.
Me interesa.	It interests me.
Lo odio.	I hate it.

Talking about obligations

To say what you have to do, use tener + que + infinitive:

Tengo que ir bien vestido.
I have to be well dressed.

Tiene que pasear al perro.
She has to walk the dog.

Useful forms of tener:

Tuve que lavar coches.
I had to wash cars.

Tenía que servir comida.
I had to serve food.

Tengo que acostarme temprano.
I have to go to bed early.

Worked example 🔊 SPEAKING

¿Tienes un trabajo a tiempo parcial?

Hago de canguro y no me gusta porque gano muy poco. Tengo que cuidar a niños traviesos y eso es difícil.

> Justifying your opinion (saying why you don't like your job) creates a subordinate clause.

AIMING HIGHER Trabajo en una cafetería a tiempo parcial para ganar dinero. Me gusta mucho trabajar con la gente pero odio despertarme antes de las doce. Ayer tuve que levantarme temprano porque trabajaba todo el día. Fue un desastre.

> Using tener que in the preterite, trabajar in the imperfect ('was working') and an opinion phrase in the preterite ('it was'), will improve your work further.

Now try this 🔊 SPEAKING

Answer this question. Speak for about one minute.

- ¿Tienes un trabajo a tiempo parcial?

Include:
- what job you do and what you have to do for it
- when you do it
- how much you earn
- whether you like it or not.

My work experience

Work experience is a good topic for showing off your knowledge of the imperfect tense.

Experiencia laboral

¿Qué experiencia laboral tienes?	What work experience have you had?
Trabajaba en ...	I was working in ...
una oficina	an office
una tienda	a shop
un instituto	a school
Hacía fotocopias.	I made photocopies.
Trabajaba con niños.	I worked with children.
Contestaba al teléfono.	I answered the phone.
Ayudaba al jefe.	I helped the boss.
Utilizaba el ordenador.	I used the computer.
Ayudaba a enfermos.	I helped sick people.

Vendía cosas a los clientes.
I sold things to customers.

Tenía que dar información a los clientes.
I had to give information to customers.

Imperfect tense: irregular verbs

 Grammar page 92

Use the imperfect tense to talk about things you used to do in the past.
Only THREE verbs are irregular in the imperfect.

	ir to go	ser to be	ver to see
I	iba	era	veía
you	ibas	eras	veías
he / she / it	iba	era	veía
we	íbamos	éramos	veíamos
you	ibais	erais	veíais
they	iban	eran	veían

Iba al trabajo en coche.
I used to go to work by car.
Era mi jefe.
He was my boss.

Worked example 🎧 51 target A

Listen. What does Fernando talk about? Put a cross in the correct box.

the other employees ☐
his journey to work ☒

– Para llegar allí, primero tenía que coger el metro y después iba a pie.

EXAM ALERT!

It's easy to make a silly mistake with questions like these. As you eliminate each answer, cross it out so that you reduce the number of possible answers.

Make sure you read the instructions and give exactly the number of answers required.

This was a real exam question that a lot of students struggled with – **be prepared!** ResultsPlus

---

Now try this 🎧 52 target A

Listen to the whole recording and put a cross in the other **three** correct boxes.

A what he did at lunchtime ☐
B the disadvantages of this kind of work ☐
C what he had to wear ☐
D what he had to do ☐
E the days he worked ☐
F the work he wants to do in the future ☐

Key vocabulary to listen out for:
• work vocabulary (empleados, tenía que, etc.)
• phrases to introduce negative opinions (no me gusta, lo peor era, etc.)
• expressions relating to the future (cuando sea mayor).

Work experience

As well as the imperfect, you'll need to know the preterite tense to talk about work experience.

Experiencia laboral

Era insoportable / repetitivo / monótono.
It was unbearable / repetitive / monotonous.

Me ayudaron mucho.
They helped me a lot.

Trabajaba muchas horas.
The hours were long.

Aprendí un montón de cosas fascinantes.
I learned a lot of exciting things.

Me trataron bien.
They treated me well.

Terminaba muy cansado.
I was very tired at the end of the day.

Los clientes eran antipáticos.
The clients were unpleasant.

Siempre había quejas.
There were always complaints.

Ojalá pudiera seguir trabajando allí.
If only I could carry on working there.

No me gustaría trabajar allí.
I wouldn't like to work there.

Imperfect or preterite?

- You use the PRETERITE tense for a SINGLE event that took place in the past.
- You use the IMPERFECT tense for repeated or CONTINUOUS actions in the past. In English we often translate them in the same way.
  Empecé a trabajar a los dieciocho anôs
  I started working at 18

Archivaba los documentos.
I filed (used to file) documents.

El jefe era un monstruo.
The boss was a monster.

Worked example 🔊 SPEAKING

¿Qué hiciste para tu experiencia laboral?

> Trabajaba en una agencia de viajes. Trabajaba muchas horas pero aprendí un montón de cosas interesantes. Terminaba muy cansado todos los días pero recibía un buen sueldo.

AIMING HIGHER
> Trabajaba en una oficina de turismo. Me encantaba trabajar con un equipo de gente tan simpática. Ayudaba a los turistas de varias nacionalidades, lo cual mejoró mucho mi nivel de inglés. Ojalá pudiera seguir trabajando allí, pero primero tendré que terminar mis estudios.

- Using two tenses (here, the **imperfect** and **preterite**) demonstrates good knowledge of language.
- Add **more detail** to improve the content level.

Using a **more complex structure** and a future tense (he states he will have to finish his studies) will really help when aiming for the top band in both content and language.

Now try this 🔊 SPEAKING

Answer this question. Speak for about one minute.
- ¿Qué experiencia laboral tienes?

Aim to include:
- where you were working
- what you were doing
- whether you liked it
- whether you would like to work there in the future.

Dialogues and messages

Learn this language to understand, take and leave phone messages.

Diálogos y mensajes

¿Sí? / Dígame.	Hello? (when answering the phone).
el prefijo	area code
Llámame / Llámeme.	Call me (informal / formal).
Le llamaré.	I'll call you (back).
Espere.	Wait.
Le paso.	I will put you through.
en la línea	on the line
de momento	at the moment
Hasta luego.	See you later.
Hasta pronto.	See you soon.
por telefóno	by phone
el contestador	voicemail

Me envia un mensaje de texto.
Send me a text.

número equivocado	wrong number
Deje un mensaje.	Leave a message.
después de la señal	after the tone
mi número de móvil	my mobile number
Si es urgente puede llamar …	If it's urgent you can call …

Worked example LISTENING 53 target A

Listen and answer the questions **in English**.

Why has the caller got Jesús's answering machine?

He's on holiday.

— ¡Hola! Ha llamado al contestador automático de Jesús. Ahora no estoy aquí porque estoy de vacaciones …

- Spanish **telephone numbers** consist of nine numbers, often starting 9 or 8 for fixed lines and 6 for mobiles. They are normally written as follows:
  657 87 42 19
  This usually would be said as: **seis, cinco, siete; ochenta y siete; cuarenta y dos; diecinueve**
- Remember: you have **five minutes** to look at the questions. You are obviously going to hear several numbers, so make sure you are prepared for that.

Now try this LISTENING 54 target A

Listen to the whole recording and answer these questions in English.

1 What other contact number does Jesús give?
2 The second answering machine message is from which company?
3 What are the opening times of the company?
4 What alternative number does the company give?

Language of the internet

Use this page to master internet language and review commands.

El lenguaje de Internet

una página digital	a web page
una contraseña	a password
descargar	to download
subir	to upload
imprimir	to print
guardar	to save
hacer click	to click
mandar	to send
recibir	to receive
un correo electrónico	an email

Giving commands

Grammar page 96

The imperative is used to give commands and instructions. It has a different form depending on whether it is POSITIVE or NEGATIVE.

mandar to send	responder to answer	subir to upload
Positive: tú form minus s		
¡Manda! Send!	¡Responde! Answer!	¡Sube! Upload!
Negative: present subjunctive		
¡No mandes! Don't send!	¡No respondas! Don't answer!	¡No subas! Don't upload.

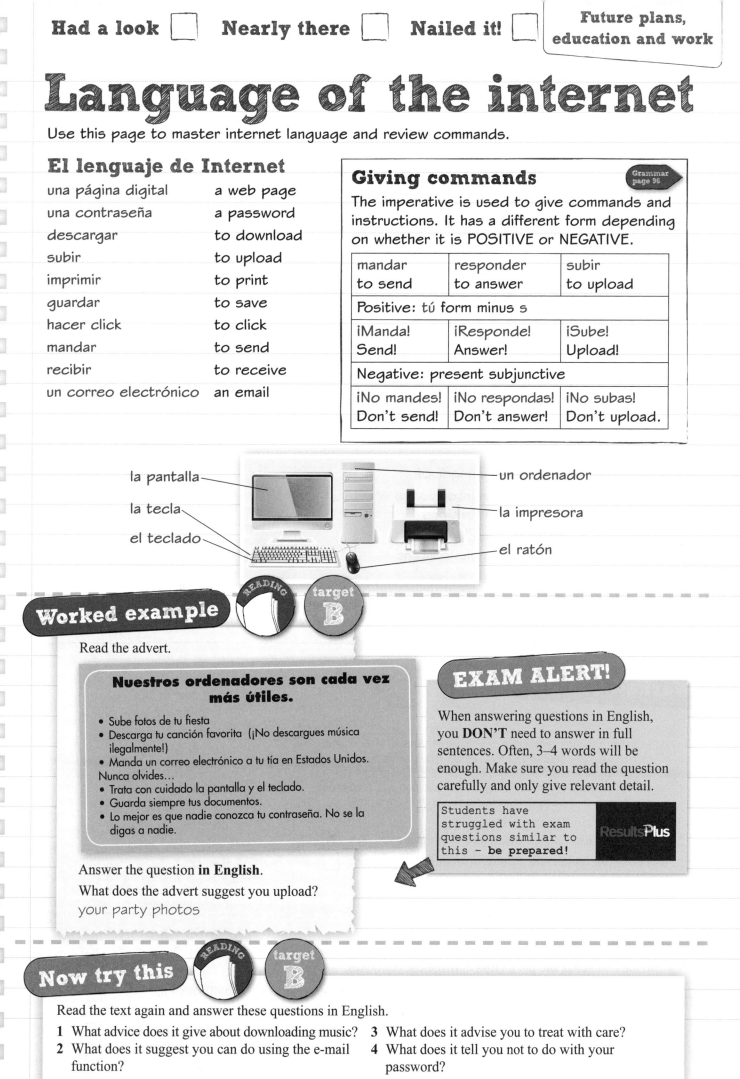

la pantalla
la tecla
el teclado
un ordenador
la impresora
el ratón

Worked example

READING   *target B*

Read the advert.

Nuestros ordenadores son cada vez más útiles.

- Sube fotos de tu fiesta
- Descarga tu canción favorita (¡No descargues música ilegalmente!)
- Manda un correo electrónico a tu tía en Estados Unidos.

Nunca olvides…
- Trata con cuidado la pantalla y el teclado.
- Guarda siempre tus documentos.
- Lo mejor es que nadie conozca tu contraseña. No se la digas a nadie.

Answer the question **in English**.

What does the advert suggest you upload?

your party photos

EXAM ALERT!

When answering questions in English, you **DON'T** need to answer in full sentences. Often, 3–4 words will be enough. Make sure you read the question carefully and only give relevant detail.

Students have struggled with exam questions similar to this – **be prepared!**

ResultsPlus

Now try this

READING   *target B*

Read the text again and answer these questions in English.

1 What advice does it give about downloading music?
2 What does it suggest you can do using the e-mail function?
3 What does it advise you to treat with care?
4 What does it tell you not to do with your password?

Internet pros and cons

Use these phrases to prepare your opinions on the internet.

Internet: las ventajas y los inconvenientes

😊

mandar y recibir mensajes
to send and to receive messages

conversar con la familia en el extranjero
to talk with family abroad

comprar y vender por Internet
to buy and to sell online

jugar a videojuegos con amigos
to play videogames with friends

leer las noticias   to read the news

☹️

el peligro de   the danger of

conocer a extraños con malas intenciones
meeting strangers with bad intentions

ver contenido inapropiado y nocivo
watching inappropriate and harmful content

el acoso escolar en las redes sociales
bullying on social networking sites

acceso a tus datos personales
access to personal data

Using ser in different tenses

Recognising ser (to be) in the past, present and future is key for higher-level reading questions.

Present	Imperfect	Future
soy	era	seré
eres	eras	serás
es	era	será

El problema más grave es la piratería informática.
The most serious problem is copyright piracy.

Escuchar y ver música por internet es guay.
Listening to and watching music online is cool.

Worked example

READING · target B

Read the article.

> Existen muchos problemas con Internet. Antes, el problema más grave era el acoso escolar en las redes sociales pero los expertos dicen que actualmente el problema más serio es la estafa en las cuentas bancarias. También dicen que dentro de diez años el contenido nocivo será el problema más grave.

- Knowing ser in the present, imperfect and future will enable you to distinguish between the problems.
- Time phrases – antes (before), actualmente (currently) and dentro de diez años (within ten years) – can also help distinguish time frames.

Put a cross by **one** correct sentence.

There are lots of problems with the internet. ☒

Online bullying is the most serious problem. ☐

Now try this

READING · target B

Read the text again and put a cross in **three** correct boxes.

1 Social networking sites are always safe. ☐

2 Fraud is now a bigger problem than online bullying. ☐

3 Bank accounts are at risk from fraud. ☐

4 In ten years, experts will solve the fraud issue. ☐

5 Fraud will always be the main problem. ☐

6 Websites with harmful content will become more of a problem. ☐

Nouns and articles

Here you'll find out about the gender of nouns and how to use the correct article.

Gender

Nouns are words that name things and people. Every Spanish noun has a gender – masculine (m) or feminine (f). If a word ends in -o or -a, it's easy to work out the gender.

ends in -o	masculine – el bolso
ends in -a	feminine – la pera

Exceptions:

el día	day	la foto	photo
el turista	tourist	la moto	motorbike
el problema	problem	la mano	hand

For words ending in any other letter, you need to learn the word with the article. If you don't know the gender, look it up in a dictionary.

cine nm cinema
↑↑
noun masculine – so **el cine**

The definite article

The definite article ('the') changes to match the gender and number of the noun.

	Singular	Plural
Masculine	el libro	los libros
Feminine	la casa	las casas

The definite article is sometimes used in Spanish when we don't use it in English:

- with abstract nouns (things you can't see / touch)

  El turismo es importante. — Tourism is important.

- with likes and dislikes

  Me gusta el francés. — I like French.

- with days of the week to say 'on'

  el domingo — on Sunday

  los domingos — on Sundays

No me gustan nada las ciencias.

I don't like science at all.

The indefinite article

The indefinite article ('a / an') changes to match the gender and number of the noun. In the plural, the English is 'some' or 'any'.

	Singular	Plural
Masculine	un libro	unos libros
Feminine	una casa	unas casas

The indefinite article is NOT used when you talk about jobs.

Soy profesor.　I'm a teacher.

Plurals

Plurals are easy to form in Spanish.

Singular	Plural
ends in a vowel un tomate	add -s unos tomates
ends in any consonant except z la región	add -es las regiones
ends in z el pez	drop z and add -ces los peces

Now try this

1 Make these nouns plural.
  1 folleto ....
  2 vez ....
  3 tradición ....
  4 café ....
  5 actor ....

2 **El** or **la**? Use a dictionary to fill in the articles.
  1 .... ciudad
  2 .... pijama
  3 .... pintor
  4 .... educación
  5 .... imagen

Adjectives

When using adjectives, you have to think about AGREEMENT and POSITION.

Adjective agreement

Adjectives describe nouns. They must agree with the noun in gender (masculine or feminine) and number (singular or plural).

Adjective	Singular	Plural
ending in -o		
masculine	alto	altos
feminine	alta	altas
ending in -e		
masculine	inteligente	inteligentes
feminine	inteligente	inteligentes
ending in a consonant		
masculine	azul	azules
feminine	azul	azules

A dictionary shows the masculine form of an adjective. Make sure you don't forget to make it agree when it's feminine and / or plural!

las faldas amarillas   the yellow skirts

Note the exceptions:

ending in -or		
masculine	hablador	habladores
feminine	habladora	habladoras
adjectives of nationality ending in s		
masculine	inglés	ingleses
feminine	inglesa	inglesas

Position of adjectives

Most Spanish adjectives come AFTER the noun.

una falda azul   a blue skirt

These adjectives always come BEFORE the noun:

mucho	a lot	próximo	next
poco	a little	último	last
primero	first	alguno	some / any
segundo	second	ninguno	none
tercero	third		

Tengo muchos amigos. I have a lot of friends.

grande comes BEFORE the noun when it means 'great' rather than 'big'. It changes to gran before both masculine and feminine singular nouns.

Fue una gran película. It was a great film.

Short forms of adjectives

Some adjectives are shortened when they come before a masculine singular noun.

bueno	good	buen
malo	bad	mal
primero	first	primer
alguno	some / any	algún
ninguno	none	ningún

Pablo es un buen amigo.

Pablo is a good friend.

Now try this

Complete the text. (Look at the adjective endings to work out where they go.)

bonitas   ruidosos   interesantes   ingleses   pequeña   habladora   históricos   simpática

Mallorca es una isla .... Tiene muchas playas .... En Mallorca hay muchos turistas .... La gente allí es muy .... y es muy .... Mallorca tiene muchos museos .... y muchos bares .... Se pueden hacer muchas cosas ....

Possessives and pronouns

Use possessives to talk about who things belong to. Using pronouns will also help you sound more fluent.

Possessive adjectives

Possessive adjectives agree with the noun they describe, NOT the owner, e.g. sus botas – his boots.

	Singular	Plural
my	mi	mis
your	tu	tus
his / her / its	su	sus
our	nuestro / a	nuestros / as
your	vuestro / a	vuestros / as
their	su	sus

mis amigos
my friends

su colegio
their school

Possessive pronouns

These agree with the noun they replace, e.g. Su chaqueta es más elegante que la mía. His jacket is smarter than mine.

	Singular	
mine	el mío	la mía
yours	el tuyo	la tuya
his / hers / its	el suyo	la suya
ours	el nuestro	la nuestra
yours	el vuestro	la vuestra
theirs	el suyo	la suya

	Plural	
mine	los míos	las mías
yours	los tuyos	las tuyas
his / hers / its	los suyos	las suyas
ours	los nuestros	las nuestras
yours	los vuestros	las vuestras
theirs	los suyos	las suyas

Prepositional pronouns

These are used after prepositions.

para – for	mí – me	nosotros / as – us
por – for	ti – you	vosotros / as – you
sin – without	él – him	ellos – them (m)
con – with	ella – her	ellas – them (f)

Esta chaqueta es para ti.
This jacket is for you.

Note the accent on mí.

con + mí ➡ conmigo   with me
con + ti ➡ contigo   with you

The relative pronoun que

que ('which', 'that' or 'who') allows you to refer back to someone or something already mentioned. You must include it in Spanish, even when you might omit it in English.

El profesor que enseña francés.
The teacher who teaches French.

El libro que lee es español.
The book (that / which) he is reading is Spanish.

Now try this

Circle the correct form each time.

Mis / Mi padrastro se llama Miguel. **Su / Sus** hijas son mis hermanastras. **Mi / Mis** hermanastra, **que / por** se llama Isabel, tiene un novio, Pablo. **Su / Sus** novio es menos guapo que **el mío / la mía**. Salgo con **él / ella** desde hace seis años. Isabel sale con **el suyo / las suyas** desde hace un mes.

Comparisons

If you're aiming for a higher grade, use structures like the comparative and superlative.

The comparative

The comparative is used to compare two things. It is formed as follows:

| más + adjective + que = more ... than |
| menos + adjective + que = less ... than |
| tan + adjective + como = as ... as |

The adjective agrees with the noun it describes.

Madrid es más interesante que Leeds.
Madrid is more interesting than Leeds.

Pablo es menos alto que su hermano.
Pablo is shorter (less tall) than his brother.

Mi habitación es tan pequeña como la tuya.
My bedroom is as small as yours.

The superlative

The superlative is used to compare more than two things. It is formed as follows:

| el / la / los / las (+ noun) + más + adjective = the most ... |
| el / la / los / las (+ noun) + menos + adjective = the least ... |

The definite article and the adjective agree with the noun described.

El español es el idioma más interesante.
Spanish is the most interesting language.

Esta casa es la menos cara del pueblo.
This house is the least expensive in the village.

Irregulars

Learn these useful irregular forms:

Adjective	Comparative	Superlative
good	better	the best
bueno	mejor	el / la mejor los / las mejores
bad	worse	the worst
malo	peor	el / la peor los / las peores

Este hotel es el mejor de la región.
This hotel is the best in the region.

Los restaurantes de aquí son los peores.
The restaurants here are the worst.

Using -ísimo for emphasis

You can add -ísimo to the end of an adjective to make it stronger.

La chaqueta es carísima.   The jacket is very expensive.

El libro es malísimo.   The book is very bad.

La comida es riquísima.
The food is really delicious.

Don't forget to make adjectives agree!

Now try this

Complete the sentences with the correct comparative or superlative.

1 Este libro es .... de la trilogía. (*worst*)
2 Mis hermanos son .... amigos que tengo. (*best*)
3 La falda es .... de la tienda. (*prettiest*)
4 Este partido de fútbol es .... (*really boring*)
5 Carmen es .... jugadora. (*best*)
6 Este piso es.............. que he visto hoy. (*ugliest*)
7 Pablo es.............. que Juan. (*better looking*)
8 Mi hermana es .... que mi hermano. (*lazier*)

Other adjectives

Here you can revise demonstrative adjectives and some useful indefinite adjectives.

Demonstrative adjectives

Demonstrative adjectives ('this', 'that', 'these', 'those') agree with their noun in number and gender.

	Masculine	Feminine	
singular	este	esta	this
plural	estos	estas	these
singular	ese	esa	that
plural	esos	esas	those

este móvil	this mobile
esa calculadora	that calculator
esos chicos	those boys
estas chicas	these girls

Using different words for 'that' and 'those'

In Spanish there are two words for 'that' / 'those': ese and aquel. You use aquel to refer to something further away.

esa chica y aquel chico

that girl and that boy (over there)

	Masculine	Feminine	
singular	aquel	aquella	that
plural	aquellos	aquellas	those

Indefinite adjectives

Indefinite adjectives come up in a lot of contexts, so make sure you know how to use them.

cada	each
otro	another
todo	all
mismo	same
algún / alguna	some / any

As with all other adjectives, remember to make them agree. Exception: **cada** – it doesn't change.

Quisiera otra cerveza.	I would like another beer.
Todos los pasajeros estaban enfadados.	All the passengers were angry.
Llevamos la misma camiseta.	We're wearing the same t-shirt.
¿Tienes algún cuaderno?	Do you have any exercise books?
Cada estudiante tiene su ordenador	Each student has their own computer.

Now try this

Translate into Spanish.

1 That boy is stupid.

2 This apple is tasty.

3 I want to buy those jeans.

4 That house over there is really big.

5 This film is boring.

6 I don't want that jumper – I want that cardigan.

Pronouns

Use pronouns to avoid repeating nouns – it helps make your Spanish more fluent and interesting.

Subject, direct object and indirect object

- The SUBJECT is the person / thing doing the action (shown by the verb).
- The OBJECT is the person / thing having the action (shown by the verb) done to it. It can be DIRECT or INDIRECT.

SUBJECT	VERB	DIRECT OBJECT	INDIRECT OBJECT
Marisa	sends	the e-mail	to David.
She	sends	it	to him.

subject pronoun		direct object pronoun		indirect object pronoun	
I	yo	me	me	(to / for) me	me
you	tú	you	te	(to / for) you	te
he / it	él	him / it	lo	(to / for) him / it	le
she / it	ella	her / it	la	(to / for) her / it	le
we	nosotros/as	us	nos	(to / for) us	nos
you	vosotros/as	you	os	(to / for) you	os
they	ellos / ellas	them	los / las	(to / for) them	les

Subject pronouns aren't often used in Spanish because the verb ending is enough to show who is doing the action. They're sometimes used for EMPHASIS.

A mí me gusta España, pero él quiere ir a Italia.   I like Spain but he wants to go to Italy.

Position of object pronouns

In general, object pronouns come:

- BEFORE the verb
- AFTER a negative

La compré en el supermercado.   I bought it in the supermarket.

No la tengo.   I don't have it.

Nadie les escribe.   No one writes to them.

The object pronoun can be added to the infinitive in the near future tense.

Voy a comprarlo por Internet.   or

Lo voy a comprar por Internet.
I'm going to buy it for my mother.

Object pronouns are attached to the end of an imperative.

¡Hazlo!   Do it!

Now try this

Rewrite the sentences, replacing the words in bold with pronouns.

1 Voy a dar **el regalo** a mi padre.

2 Quiero **a mi hermana**.

3 Voy a comprar **un libro**.

4 Vi **a Katie y Ryan** en Bilbao.

5 Quiero decir **a Pablo** un secreto.

The present tense

This page covers all three types of regular verbs and stem-changing verbs in the present tense.

Present tense (regular)

To form the present tense of regular verbs, replace the infinitive ending as follows:

	hablar – to speak	comer – to eat	vivir – to live
I	hablo	como	vivo
you	hablas	comes	vives
he / she / it	habla	come	vive
we	hablamos	comemos	vivimos
you	habláis	coméis	vivís
they	hablan	comen	viven

How to use the present tense

Use the present tense to talk about:
- what are you are doing NOW
- what you do REGULARLY
- what things are LIKE.

You can also use the present tense to talk about planned future events.

Mañana voy a España.   Tomorrow I'm going to Spain.

Recognise and use a range of present tense time expressions, e.g.

ahora	now
hoy	today
en este momento	at this moment
los martes	on Tuesdays.

Stem-changing verbs

In stem-changing verbs, the vowel in the syllable before the infinitive ending changes in the singular and 3rd person plural. There are three common groups.

	o ➡ ue poder to be able	e ➡ ie querer to want	e ➡ i pedir to ask
I	puedo	quiero	pido
you	puedes	quieres	pides
he / she / it	puede	quiere	pide
we	podemos	queremos	pedimos
you	podéis	queréis	pedís
they	pueden	quieren	piden

Other examples of stem-changing verbs:

u / o ➡ ue	e ➡ ie
jugar ➡ juego play	empezar ➡ empiezo start
dormir ➡ duermo sleep	entender ➡ entiendo understand
volver ➡ vuelvo return	pensar ➡ pienso think
encontrar ➡ encuentro meet	preferir ➡ prefiero prefer

¿Quieres salir esta noche?
Do you want to go out tonight?
Rafa juega al tenis todos los días.
Rafa plays tennis every day.

Now try this

Complete the sentences using the present tense.

1 No .... música clásica. *escuchar (I)*
2 Mis padres .... inglés. *hablar*
3 Mi amigo .... al baloncesto conmigo. *jugar*
4 ¿............... ir al cine conmigo esta noche? *querer (you singular informal)*
5 Siempre .... fruta para estar sanos. *comer (we)*
6 Siempre .... dinero en la calle. *encontrar (they)*
7 ¿............... en el campo? *vivir (you plural informal)*
8 Mi hermano .... en su propio dormitorio. *dormir*

Reflexives and irregulars

Reflexive verbs include a reflexive pronoun which refers back to the person doing the action.

Present tense (regular)

Reflexive verbs have the same endings as other present tense verbs but contain a reflexive pronoun. Some are also stem-changing verbs.

	lavarse to wash	vestirse to get dressed
I	me lavo	me visto
you	te lavas	te vistes
he / she / it	se lava	se viste
we	nos lavamos	nos vestimos
you	os laváis	os vestís
they	se lavan	se visten

In the infinitive form, the pronoun can be added to the end of the verb.

Voy a levantarme.   I'm going to get up.

Useful reflexive verbs

Reflexive verbs are particularly useful when you're talking about daily routine.

acostarse	Me acuesto.	I go to bed.
afeitarse	Me afeito.	I shave.
despertarse	Me despierto.	I wake up.
ducharse	Me ducho.	I have a shower.
levantarse	Me levanto.	I get up.
peinarse	Me peino.	I comb my hair.

Me visto.   Me cepillo los dientes.

The verbs ir and haber

These are irregular in the present tense.

	ir – to go	haber – to have
I	voy	he
you	vas	has
he / she / it	va	ha / hay
we	vamos	hemos
you	vais	habéis
they	van	han / hay

Other irregular verbs

Some verbs are irregular in the 'I' form only.

conducir	to drive	➡ conduzco
conocer	to know / meet	➡ conozco
dar	to give	➡ doy
hacer	to make / do	➡ hago
poner	to put	➡ pongo
saber	to know	➡ sé
salir	to go out	➡ salgo
tener	to have	➡ tengo
traer	to bring	➡ traigo

Now try this

1 Complete the sentences with the correct reflexive pronouns.

1 .... despierto temprano.

2 Mi hermano .... afeita a las siete.

3 Mañana voy a peinar .... antes de desayunar.

4 .... acostamos siempre a la misma hora.

5 ¿A qué hora .... levantas normalmente?

6 Mis padres .... duchan después de desayunar.

2 Unscramble the verbs and translate them into English.

1 zoncoco   ....

2 goten   ....

3 somav   ....

4 gnoop   ....

5 olgas   ....

6 oagrit   ....

Ser and estar

Spanish has two verbs meaning 'to be': ser and estar. Both are irregular – you need to know them well.

The present tense of ser

	ser – to be
I am	soy
you are	eres
he / she / it is	es
we are	somos
you are	sois
they are	son

Roberto es un chico feliz.
Roberto is a happy boy.

When to use ser

Use ser for PERMANENT things.

* nationality
Soy inglés.   I'm English.
* occupation
Es profesor.   He's a teacher.
* colour and size
Es rojo. Es pequeño.   It's red. It's small.
* personality
Son habladoras.   They're talkative.
* telling the time
Son las tres.   It's three o'clock.

The present tense of estar

	estar – to be
I am	estoy
you are	estás
he / she / it is	está
we are	estamos
you are	estáis
they are	están

Hoy Alicia está aburridísima.

Alicia is really bored today.

When to use estar

Use estar for TEMPORARY things and LOCATIONS.

* illness
Estoy enfermo.   I'm unwell.
* appearance (temporary)
Estás guapo.   You look handsome.
* feelings (temporary)
Estoy contento porque gané la lotería.
I'm happy because I won the lottery.
* location
Madrid está en   Madrid is in Spain.
España.

Watch out for this one!
ser listo   to be clever
estar listo   to be ready

Now try this

Complete the sentences with **ser** or **estar** in the present tense.

1 ¿Dónde .... la parada de autobuses?

2 Valencia .... grande e interesante.

3 Mi hermano .... abogado.

4 .... constipado. (I)

5 Las botas .... negras.

6 Mi mejor amiga .... escocesa.

7 Hoy mis amigos no .... contentos porque tienen una prueba.

8 María .... guapa esta noche con su vestido nuevo.

The gerund

Gerunds are '–ing' words. Use this page to review how they're formed and used.

The gerund

To form the gerund of regular verbs, replace the infinitive ending as follows:

hablar – hablando

comer – comiendo

vivir – viviendo

Common irregular gerunds:

caer	cayendo	falling
dormir	durmiendo	sleeping
leer	leyendo	reading
oír	oyendo	hearing
pedir	pidiendo	asking (for something)
poder	pudiendo	being able to
reír	riendo	laughing

Está jugando a fútbol.
He's playing football.

Uses of the gerund

You use the gerund:

- to give more information about how something was or is being done

  e.g. Voy andando al instituto.

  I go to school on foot.

- after ir (to go), seguir (to keep on) and continuar (to continue)

  Sigo aprendiendo informática porque es útil.

  I keep studying ICT because it's useful.

- to form the present continuous and imperfect continuous tenses (see below).

You can't always translate an '-ing' verb in English by the gerund in Spanish, e.g.
Aprender español es emocionante.
Learning Spanish is exciting.
Vamos a salir mañana.
We're leaving tomorrow.

Present continuous tense

The present continuous describes what is happening at this moment:

present tense of estar + the gerund

	estar – to be	gerund
I	estoy	
you	estás	haciendo
he / she / it	está	saliendo
we	estamos	durmiendo
you	estáis	riendo
they	están	

Estoy viendo la televisión. I'm watching TV.

Imperfect continuous tense

This tense describes what was happening at a certain moment in the past:

imperfect tense of estar + the gerund

	estar – to be	gerund
I	estaba	
you	estabas	visitando
he / she / it	estaba	estudiando
we	estábamos	escribiendo
you	estabais	buscando
they	estaban	

Estaba leyendo. I was reading.

Now try this

Rewrite the sentences using the present continuous tense. Write them again using the imperfect continuous.

1 Juego al tenis.

2 Escribo un correo electrónico.

3 Habla con mi amigo Juan.

4 Duerme en la cama.

5 Como cereales.

6 Tomo el sol en la playa

7 Navegan por internet.

8 ¿Cantas en tu habitación?

The preterite tense

The preterite tense is used to talk about completed actions in the past.

Preterite tense (regular)

To form the preterite tense of regular verbs, replace the infinitive ending as follows:

	hablar – to speak	comer – to eat	vivir – to live
I	hablé	comí	viví
you	hablaste	comiste	viviste
he / she / it	habló	comió	vivió
we	hablamos	comimos	vivimos
you	hablasteis	comisteis	vivisteis
they	hablaron	comieron	vivieron

Be careful – accents can be significant.
Hablo. I speak.
Habló. He / She spoke.

How to use the preterite tense

You use the preterite to describe completed actions in the past.

El año pasado viajé a Estados Unidos.
Last year I travelled to the United States.

Recognise and use a range of preterite tense time expressions,

ayer	yesterday
anoche	last night
anteayer / antes de ayer	the day before yesterday
el verano pasado	last summer
la semana pasada	last week

Preterite tense (irregular)

	ir – to go ser – to be	hacer – to do	ver – to see
yo	fui	hice	vi
tú	fuiste	hiciste	viste
él/ella	fue	hizo	vio
nosotros/as	fuimos	hicimos	vimos
vosotros/as	fuisteis	hicisteis	visteis
ellos/as	fueron	hicieron	vieron

The verbs **ir** and **ser** have the same forms in the preterite. Use context to work out which is meant.

Useful irregular preterite forms to know:

dar	di	I gave
estar	estuve	I was
saber	supe	I knew
andar	anduve	I walked
venir	vine	I came
poner	puse	I put
decir	dije	I said

Note these verbs with irregular spelling in 'I' form only:

tocar	toqué	I played
cruzar	crucé	I crossed
empezar	empecé	I started
jugar	jugué	I played
llegar	llegué	I arrived

Now try this

Identify the tense in each sentence (present or preterite). Then translate the sentences into English.

1 Voy a Italia.
2 Llegué a las seis.
3 Navego por Internet.
4 Escuchó música.
5 Fue a una fiesta que fue guay.
6 Hizo frío y llovió un poco.
7 Vimos a Pablo en el mercado.
8 Jugué al baloncesto en la playa.

The imperfect tense

The imperfect is another verb tense used to talk about the past.

Imperfect tense (regular)

To form the imperfect tense of regular verbs, replace the infinitive ending as follows:

	hablar – to speak	comer – to eat	vivir – to live
I	hablaba	comía	vivía
you	hablabas	comías	vivías
he / she / it	hablaba	comía	vivía
we	hablábamos	comíamos	vivíamos
you	hablabais	comíais	vivíais
they	hablaban	comían	vivían

–er and –ir verbs have the same endings.

Aim to use both the **imperfect** and the **preterite** in your work to aim for a higher grade.

How to use the imperfect tense

You use the imperfect to talk about:

- what people USED TO DO / how things USED TO BE

  Antes no separaba la basura.
  I didn't use to sort the rubbish before.

- REPEATED ACTIONS in the past

  Jugaba al tenis todos los días.
  I played tennis every day.

- DESCRIPTIONS in the past

  El hotel era caro.
  The hotel was expensive.

Hacía de canguro. Ahora trabajo como jardinera.
I used to babysit. Now I work as a gardener.

Imperfect tense (irregular)

Only three verbs are irregular:

	ir – to go	ser – to be	ver – to see
I	iba	era	veía
you	ibas	eras	veías
he / she / it	iba	era	veía
we	íbamos	éramos	veíamos
you	ibais	erais	veíais
they	iban	eran	veían

Preterite or imperfect?

- Use the preterite tense for a SINGLE / COMPLETED event in the past.
- Use the imperfect tense for REPEATED / CONTINUOUS events in the past.

  En Brighton había un castillo.
  There used to be a castle in Brighton.

  Ayer visité Brighton.
  Yesterday I visited Brighton.

Now try this

Complete the sentences with the imperfect or preterite tense, as appropriate.

1 Mi madre .... para Iberia todos los veranos. *trabajar*

2 Ayer .... mucho chocolate. *comer* (I eat)

3 Antes .... a Grecia a menudo con mis padres. *ir* (I go)

4 En los años setenta .... más paro que ahora. *haber*

5 El verano pasado .... Marruecos por primera vez. *visitar* (I visit)

6 De pequeño mi hermanito .... siempre. *llorar*

The future tense

To aim for a higher grade, you need to use a future tense as well as the present and past.

Future tense

To form the future tense of most verbs, add the following endings to the infinitive:

ir – to go			
I	iré	we	iremos
you	irás	you	iréis
he / she / it	irá	they	irán

Some verbs use a different stem. You need to memorise these:

decir to say	➡	diré I will say
hacer to make / do	➡	haré I will make / do
poder to be able to	➡	podré I will be able to
querer to want	➡	querré I will want
saber to know	➡	sabré I will know
salir to leave	➡	saldré I will leave
tener to have	➡	tendré I will have
venir to come	➡	vendré I will come
haber there is / are	➡	habré there will be

Near future tense

You form the near future tense as follows:

present tense of ir + a + infinitive

	ir – to go		infinitive
I	voy		
you	vas		mandar
he / she / it	va	a	bailar
we	vamos		salir
you	vais		venir
they	van		

¿Vas a comer algo?
Are you going to have something to eat?

Vamos a ir a la fiesta.
We're going to go to the festival.

Recognise and use a range of time expressions that indicate the future, e.g. mañana tomorrow, mañana por la mañana tomorrow morning, el mes que viene next month, el próximo viernes next Friday.

Using the future tense

Use the future tense to talk about what WILL happen in the future.

El año que viene será difícil encontrar un buen trabajo.
Next year it will be difficult to find a good job.

Si trabajo como voluntario, mejoraré el mundo.
If I work as a volunteer, I will make the world better.

Using the near future tense

You use the near future tense to say what is going to happen. It is used to talk about future plans.

En Barcelona va a comprar recuerdos.
He's going to buy souvenirs in Barcelona.

Voy a salir esta tarde.
I'm going to leave this afternoon.

Now try this

1 Rewrite the sentences using the future tense.
   1 Nunca fumo.
   2 Ayudo a los demás.
   3 Cambiamos el mundo.
   4 Trabajo en un aeropuerto.

2 Rewrite the sentences using the near future tense.
   1 Salgo a las seis.
   2 Soy médico.
   3 Va a España.
   4 Mañana juego al tenis.

The conditional

The conditional is used to describe what you WOULD DO or what WOULD HAPPEN in the future.

The conditional

To form the conditional, you add the following endings to the infinitive:

	hablar – to speak
I	hablaría
you	hablarías
he / she / it	hablaría
we	hablaríamos
you	hablaríais
they	hablarían

The endings are the same for ALL verbs.

Some verbs use a different stem.

decir to say	➡	diría
hacer to do	➡	haría
poder to be able to	➡	podría
querer to want	➡	querría
saber to know	➡	sabría
salir to leave	➡	saldría
tener to have	➡	tendría
venir to come	➡	vendría
haber there is / are	➡	habría

Un sistema de alquiler de bicicletas sería una idea muy buena.
A bike hire scheme would be a really good idea.

Use **poder** in the conditional + the infinitive to say what you COULD do.
Podríamos ir a Ibiza.   We could go to Ibiza.

Use **deber** in the conditional + the infinitive to say what you SHOULD do.
Debería fumar menos cigarrillos.
I should smoke fewer cigarettes.

Expressing future intent

The conditional can be used to express future intent. Use gustar in the conditional + the infinitive.

En el futuro ...

me gustaría ir a Australia.
I'd love to go to Australia

me gustaría ser bailadora.
I'd love to be a dancer

me gustaría comprar un coche nuevo.
I'd like to buy a new car

You can also use me encantaría, e.g. Me encantaría ser futbolista.

Now try this

Rewrite the text, changing the verbs in bold to the conditional.

Para mantenerme en forma **bebo** mucha agua. **Hago** mucho ejercicio y **practico** mucho deporte. Nunca **tomo** drogas y no **bebo** alcohol. **Como** mucha fruta y **me acuesto** temprano – siempre **duermo** ocho horas, gracias a eso **llevo** una vida sana.

Perfect and pluperfect

The perfect and pluperfect are two more tenses used to talk about the past. You should be able to use both.

Perfect tense

To form the perfect tense, use the present tense of haber + past participle:

	haber – to have
I	he
you	has
he / she / it	ha
we	hemos
you	habéis
they	han

Pluperfect tense

To form the pluperfect tense, use the imperfect tense of haber + past participle:

	haber – to have
I	había
you	habías
he / she / it	había
we	habíamos
you	habíais
they	habían

Past participle

To form the past participle, replace the infinitive ending as follows:

hablar – hablado

comer – comido

vivir – vivido

Ha comprado un nuevo CD.   He has bought a new CD.
No habían salido.   They hadn't gone out.
Había hecho mis deberes.   I had done my homework.
¿Has visto a María?   Have you seen María?

Here are some common irregular past participles:

abrir	abierto	➡ opened
decir	dicho	➡ said
escribir	escrito	➡ written
hacer	hecho	➡ done
poner	puesto	➡ put
romper	roto	➡ broken
ver	visto	➡ seen
volver	vuelto	➡ returned

Using the perfect tense

The perfect tense describes what someone HAS DONE or something that HAS HAPPENED.

He ido a la piscina.
I have been to the swimming pool.

Using the pluperfect tense

The pluperfect tense describes what someone HAD DONE or something that HAD HAPPENED at a particular time in the past.

Cuando llegó, la orquesta había empezado ya.

When he arrived, the orchestra had already started.

Now try this

Rewrite the sentences in the correct order. Identify the tense in each one: perfect or pluperfect?

1 visitado / he / . / novio / mi / con / Palma
2 ayuda / hecho / deberes / mi / . / han / sus / con
3 ido / . / habíamos / Pablo / con / supermercado / al
4 amor / de / carta / una / . / escrito / ha / hermana / mi
5 has / ¿ / abrigo / mi / visto / ?
6 llegó / cuando / , / primos / ya / comido / . / mis / habían /

Giving instructions

You use the imperative to give INSTRUCTIONS and COMMANDS.

The imperative

The imperative has a different form depending on:

• who is receiving the command

• whether the command is positive or negative.

> Formal commands use the 3rd person forms of the present subjunctive for both positive and negative – see page 79.

POSITIVE IMPERATIVES (INFORMAL)

escuchar – to listen	correr – to run	abrir – to open
To one person: present tense –'you' singular minus s		
¡Escucha! Listen!	¡Corre! Run!	¡Abre! Open!
To more than one person: infinitive with final r changed to d		
¡Escuchad! Listen!	¡Corred! Run!	¡Abrid! Open!

NEGATIVE IMPERATIVES (INFORMAL)

To one person: present subjunctive – 'you' singular		
¡No escuches! Don't listen!	¡No corras! Don't run!	¡No abras! Don't open!
To more than one person: present subjunctive – 'you' plural		
¡No escuchéis! Don't listen!	¡No corráis! Don't run!	¡No abráis! Don't open!

Irregular imperatives

These verbs have irregular imperatives in the 'you' singular form.

decir	➡	¡Di!	Say!
hacer	➡	¡Haz!	Do!
ir	➡	¡Ve!	Go!
dar	➡	¡Da!	Give!
salir	➡	¡Sal!	Leave!
tener	➡	¡Ten!	Have!

How to use the imperative

The imperative is used to give commands and instructions.

Toma la primera calle a la izquierda.
Take the first street on the left.

Poned la mesa, por favor.
Set the table, please.

¡No hables!
Don't talk!

Now try this

Translate the instructions into English.

1 Escríbeme.

2 Espera a tu hermana.

3 No me digas.

4 ¡No gritéis!

5 Haz clic aquí.

6 ¡No saques fotos!

7 Contestad las preguntas.

8 No dejes todo para último momento.

¡No saques fotos!

The present subjunctive

The subjunctive form of the verb is used in certain constructions.

The present subjunctive

To form the present subjunctive, replace the −o ending of the 'I' form of the present tense as follows:

	hablar to speak	comer to eat	vivir to live
I	hable	coma	viva
you	hables	comas	vivas
he / she / it	hable	coma	viva
we	hablemos	comamos	vivamos
you	habléis	comáis	viváis
they	hablen	coman	vivan

-er and -ir verbs have the same endings.

This rule works for most verbs which are irregular in the present tense.

Infinitive	Present	Subjunctive
hacer	hago	haga
tener	tengo	tenga

Two verbs, ir and ser, are different.

	ir – to go	ser – to be
I	vaya	sea
you	vayas	seas
he / she / it	vaya	sea
we	vayamos	seamos
you	vayáis	seáis
they	vayan	sean

How to use the subjunctive

The subjunctive is used:

- to express doubt or uncertainty

No creo que tenga tiempo.
I don't think I have time.

- after ojalá

¡Ojalá (que) nadie me vea!
Let's hope no one sees me!

- to express a wish with querer que

¿Quieres que nos vayamos?
Do you want us to go?

- to express a negative opinion

No es verdad que sea adicto al ordenador.
It isn't true that I'm a computer addict.

- after cuando when talking about the future

Cuando sea mayor, quiero hacer caída libre.
When I'm older, I want to do skydiving.

Remember: the subjunctive is also used in some imperatives – see page 96.

Now try this

Translate the sentences into English.

1 Cuando vaya a la universidad, estudiaré francés.
2 No creo que tu amigo sea guapo.
3 Cuando tenga dieciocho años, me tomaré un año sabático.
4 Quiero que hables con Pablo.
5 No es verdad que la comida inglesa sea horrible.
6 No creo que Italia sea el mejor equipo de fútbol.

It's important you can **recognise** the subjunctive. If you're really aiming high, you could also try to **use** a few subjunctive forms in your writing and speaking.

Negatives

You need to be able to understand and use negatives in all parts of the exam.

Negatives

no	not
no … nada	nothing / not anything
no … nunca	never
no … jamás	never
no … ni … ni …	not … (either) … or …
no … tampoco	not … either
no … ningún / ninguna	no / not any
no … nadie	no one

No tengo nada que ponerme.
I don't have anything to wear.

No quiero ni nadar ni hacer yoga.
I don't want to swim or do yoga.

No me gustan los perros tampoco.
I don't like dogs either.

How to use negatives

- The simplest way to make a sentence negative in Spanish is to use no. It comes before the verb.

  No nadé en el mar.
  I didn't swim in the sea.

- Negative expressions with two parts sandwich the verb (i.e. they go round it).

  Dicen que no nieva nunca en Málaga.
  They say that it never snows in Malaga.

- Two-part negative expressions can be shortened and put before the verb for emphasis.

  Nadie está aquí. No one's here.

Expressions to use with negatives

Ya no estudio alemán.	I no longer study German.
No bebo agua sino zumo de naranja.	I don't drink water but orange juice.
Todavía no ha estudiado mucho.	He hasn't studied a lot yet.
Espero que no.	I hope not.
Creo que no.	I don't think so.
Claro que no.	Of course not.

Use a range of negatives in your Spanish to aim for a higher grade.

Now try this

Make the sentences negative, giving the opposite meanings.

1 Siempre como verduras.

2 Tengo un libro.

3 Conozco a todos sus amigos.

4 Todo el mundo juega a pelota.

5 Siempre hago mis deberes.

6 Me gusta navegar por Internet y descargar música.

7 Tiene todo.

8 Tengo muchos amigos en Londres.

Special verbs

Verbs like gustar are used mainly in the 3rd person. You'll need them for a lot of topics, so they're worth learning carefully.

Present tense of gustar

Me gusta ('I like') literally translates as 'it pleases me'. The thing that does the pleasing (i.e. the thing I like) is the subject.

Me gusta este libro.   I like this book.

If the subject is plural, use me gustan.

Me gustan estos libros. I like these books.

The pronoun changes as follows:

me	gusta(n)	I like
te	gusta(n)	you like
le	gusta(n)	he / she / it likes
nos	gusta(n)	we like
os	gusta(n)	you like
les	gusta(n)	they like

To talk about other people's likes / dislikes, you need a before their name:

A Ignacio le gusta el deporte. Ignacio likes sport.

Preterite tense of gustar

In the preterite:

me gusta ➡ me gustó

me gustan ➡ me gustaron

The pronouns in the other forms are the same as for the present tense.

Nos gustó la comida española.
We liked Spanish food.

Le gustaron las tiendas.
She liked the shops.

If you're aiming for higher grades, use gustar in the preterite to extend your language range.

encantar behaves in the same way as gustar:
Le encanta la música rock. He loves rock music.

Other verbs like gustar

Other verbs follow the same pattern as gustar: pronoun + 3rd person singular / plural of the verb

doler	me duelen(n)	My ... hurt(s)
quedar	me queda(n)	I have ... left
hacer falta	me hace(n) falta	I need ...
faltar	me falta	I'm missing ...

Me duele el tobillo.
My ankle hurts.

Les quedan 20 euros.
They have 20 euros left.

¿Te hace falta una cuchara?
Do you need a spoon?

Le faltan dos libros.
He's missing two books.

Now try this

Complete the sentences.

1 .... el brazo. (doler, I)

2 .... el queso. (gustar, she)

3 .... los españoles. (gustar, I, preterite)

4 .... un cuchillo. (hacer falta, they)

5 .... los pies. (doler, he)

6 .... el español. (encantar, I)

7 .... cinco euros. (quedar, we)

8 .... las películas francesas. (gustar, María)

Por and para

Por and para are both often translated by 'for' in English. Learn the different contexts in which they're used.

Using por

You use por for:

- CAUSE
  Pagué cien euros por el vuelo.
  I paid €100 for the flight.
  El vuelo está cancelado por la huelga.
  The flight was cancelled because of the strike.

- to indicate action ON BEHALF OF someone
  Lo hizo por mí. She did it for me.

- when expressing RATES
  Gano seis euros por hora.
  I earn €6 per hour.

- means of COMMUNICATION
  Me llamó por teléfono.
  He called me on the phone.

- periods of TIME
  Me quedaré en Barcelona por poco tiempo.
  I will stay in Barcelona for a short time.

Using para

You use para for:

- PURPOSE (it can often be translated by 'in order to')
  Llevamos una botella de agua fría para el viaje.
  We're taking a bottle of cold water for the journey.
  Voy a utilizar mi tarjeta de crédito para pagar el hotel.
  I'm going to use my credit card to pay for the hotel.
  Voy a comprar unos regalos para mi familia.
  I'm going to buy some presents for my family.

- DESTINATION
  Ha salido para Bilbao.
  She has left for Bilbao.

- periods of TIME in the future
  Quisiera una habitación para quince días.
  I would like a room for a fortnight.

Try writing out phrases with **por** and **para**, using one colour for **por** each time and another colour for **para**. Then when you're trying to remember which one to use, try to visualise the colour.

Now try this

1 Choose **por** or **para** to complete these sentences.

  1 Voy a ir a Madrid .... hacer compras.

  2 El tren .... Sevilla sale a las seis.

  3 Gracias .... el regalo.

  4 Los deberes son .... mañana.

  5 Este regalo es .... mi profesor.

  6 Voy a llamarle .... teléfono.

  7 Una azafata gana veinte euros .... hora.

2 Tick the sentences which are correct. Correct those that are wrong.

  1 Salimos por Nueva York.

  2 Solo estudio para la mañana.

  3 Por ganar hay que trabajar duro.

  4 Voy a hacerlo para ti.

  5 Juego al fútbol para divertirme.

  6 Estas flores son por mi novia.

  7 Ganar dinero para vender tu móvil viejo.

  8 En 18 por ciento de las casas hay una motocicleta.

Questions and exclamations

Being able to use questions and exclamations is essential in most topics.

How to ask questions

To ask yes / no questions, use the same language as you would to say the sentence and:

- if you're writing, add question marks
- if you're speaking, use a rising intonation at the end.

¿Estudias español?
Do you study Spanish?

¿Quieres ir al polideportivo?
Do you want to go to the leisure centre?

Remember the ¿ at the start.

To ask open questions, use a question word.

¿Cuándo?	When?
¿Dónde?	Where?
¿Adónde?	Where to?
¿De dónde?	From where?
¿Cuánto / a?	How much?
¿Cuántos / as?	How many?
¿Qué?	What?
¿Por qué?	Why?
¿Cómo?	How?
¿Cuál(es)?	Which (ones)?
¿Quién(es)?	Who?
¿Cuál (de estos libros) te gusta más?	Which (one of these books) do you like more?

Don't forget the accents on question words.

Using exclamations

Using exclamations is a good way to extend how you give opinions in your spoken and written Spanish. Here are some useful examples:

¡Qué lástima!	What a shame!
¡Qué problema!	What a problem!
¡Qué raro!	How strange!
¡Qué va!	No way!
¡Qué rollo!	How boring!

Remember the ¡ at the start as well as at the end.

¡Qué emocionante!
How exciting!

¡Qué difícil!
How difficult!

Question tag

English has a lot of different ways of asking for confirmation, e.g. 'doesn't he?', 'haven't they?', 'can't you?'. In Spanish it's much easier. You just put verdad at the end of a question.

¿Pablo es tu novio, verdad?
Pablo is your boyfriend, isn't he?

Now try this

Match the sentence halves.

1 ¿Cuál   a cuesta?
2 ¿Adónde   b personas hay en tu clase?
3 ¿Quién   c te llamas?
4 ¿Dónde   d es tu asignatura preferida?
5 ¿Cuánto   e está Jaén?
6 ¿Cuántas   f fuiste de vacaciones el año pasado?
7 ¿Cómo   g es tu cumpleaños?
8 ¿Cuándo   h es tu pintor preferido?

Connectives and adverbs

Use connectives to link phrases and sentences, and use adverbs to add detail to your Spanish.

Connectives

Connectives are words that link phrases and sentences together. You can use them to make your Spanish more varied and interesting.

Hago atletismo pero no me gusta mucho.

I do athletics but I don't like it much.

ademas	as well / besides
antes (de)	before
así que	so / therefore
después (de)	after
entonces	then
mientras	while
o	or
pero	but
porque	because
por desgracia	unfortunately
por eso	therefore
por una parte	on the one hand
por otra parte	on the other hand
pues	then
si	if
sin embargo	however
también	also
y	and

Another good way to improve your work is to extend your sentences using clauses with: **que** that / who, **donde** where, **cuando** when, **como** like / as, **cuyo** whose.

Adverbs

Adverbs describe how an action is done – they give you more detail about verbs.

They are formed by adding -mente to the feminine form of the adjective

lento ➡ lenta ➡ lentamente   slowly

Adverbs usually come AFTER the verb.

Monta a caballo frecuentemente.
She goes riding frequently.

Sometimes they come BEFORE the verb, for emphasis.

Siempre nado los martes.
I always go swimming on Tuesdays.

Irregular adverbs

Here are some useful irregular adverbs to learn:

bastante	enough	despacio	slow
bien	well	mal	badly
demasiado	too	mucho	a lot
	much	poco	a little
deprisa	fast	ya	already

Now try this

1 Connect the sentence pairs with an appropriate connective.

  1 Nunca voy a Paris. Es aburrido.

  2 Jugaba al baloncesto. Juan hacía patinaje.

  3 Estudiar. Iré a la universidad.

  4 Nos gustaría ir a la playa. Está lloviendo.

2 Make adverbs from the adjectives. Translate them into English.

  1 tranquilo

  2 perfecto

  3 dificil

  4 severo

Numbers

Numbers come up in almost EVERY context. Make sure you know them well.

Numbers

1	uno	11	once	21	veintiuno	100	cien
2	dos	12	doce	22	veintidós	101	ciento uno
3	tres	13	trece	30	treinta	200	doscientos / as
4	cuatro	14	catorce	31	treinta y uno	333	trescientos / as
5	cinco	15	quince	32	treinta y dos		treinta y tres
6	seis	16	dieciséis	40	cuarenta	1000	mil
7	siete	17	diecisiete	50	cincuenta		
8	ocho	18	dieciocho	60	sesenta		
9	nueve	19	diecinueve	70	setenta		
10	diez	20	veinte	80	ochenta		
				90	noventa		

> The hundreds need to agree. Note: there are some irregular forms:
> 500 – quinientos,
> 700 – setecientos,
> 900 – novecientos.

> The pattern for 31, 32, etc., is the same for 41, 42, etc.

Ordinal numbers

When used with nouns, ordinal numbers agree.

primero	first	sexto	sixth
segundo	second	séptimo	seventh
tercero	third	octavo	eighth
cuarto	fourth	noveno	ninth
quinto	fifth	décimo	tenth

Primero and tercero change to primer and tercer before a masculine singular noun, e.g. el tercer día.

> Ordinals are NOT used for dates except for the 1st.

Telling the time

Son las cinco.	It's five o'clock.
A las diez.	At ten o'clock.

> One o'clock is different: Es la una.

3.05	las tres y cinco
3.15	las tres y cuarto
3.30	las tres y media
3.45	las cuatro menos cuarto
3.55	las cuatro menos cinco

Dates

Dates follow this pattern:

13 December 1978 =

el trece de diciembre de mil novecientos setenta y ocho

The first of the month can be either:
el primero de abril or el uno de abril.

> You don't use a capital letter for the months.

Now try this

Write the numbers, dates and times in Spanish.

(a) 8.40 (b) 465 (c) 12 June 2014 (d) 7th (e) 11.30 (f) 76 (g) 1 January 1997 (h) 3rd

103

Vocabulary

This section starts with general terms that are useful in a wide variety of situations and then divides into vocabulary for each of the four main topics covered in this revision guide:

1 High frequency language   **2** Personal information   **3** Out and about

4 Customer service and transactions   **5** Future plans, education and work

F Sections to be learnt by all candidates   **H** Sections to be learnt by Higher candidates only

Learning vocabulary is essential preparation for your reading and listening exams. Don't try to learn too much at once – concentrate on learning and testing yourself on a page at a time.

1 High frequency language

Verbs A–C		Verbs D–H		Verbs I–P	
abrir	to open	dar	to give	ir de compras	to go shopping
acabar	to finish	darse prisa	to hurry	ir	to go
aceptar	to accept	deber	to have to	lavar(se)	to wash (oneself)
acompañar	to accompany	decir	to say	leer	to read
aconsejar	to advise	dejar	to leave (object)	levantarse	to get up
acostarse	to go to bed	desayunar	to have breakfast	llamar	to call
afeitarse	to shave	descargar	to download	llamarse	to be called
agradecer	to thank	(música)	(music)	llegar	to arrive
ahorrar	to save (money)	desear	to wish	llevar	to carry, wear
almorzar	to have lunch	dibujar	to draw	llevarse bien	to get on well
alquilar	to rent, hire	discutir	to discuss	con	with
amar	to love	disfrutar	to enjoy	llorar	to cry
andar	to walk	divertirse	to enjoy oneself	llover	to rain
añadir	to add	doler	to hurt	mandar	to send
aprender	to learn	dormir	to sleep	maquillarse	to put on make up
arreglar	to tidy	ducharse	to shower	montar (a	to ride (a horse)
ayudar	to help	durar	to last	caballo)	
bailar	to dance	echar de	to miss	morir	to die
bajar	to get off (a bus)	menos		nacer	to be born
bañarse	to bathe	elegir	to choose	nadar	to swim
beber	to drink	empezar	to begin	navegar en	to surf the
buscar	to look for	encantar	to love	internet	internet
caer	to fall	encontrar	to meet	nevar	to snow
cambiar	to change	enfadarse	to get angry	odiar	to hate
cantar	to sing	enseñar	to show, teach	ofrecer	to give (presents)
cenar	to have dinner	entender	to understand	(regalos)	
cepillarse	to brush (teeth, hair)	enviar	to send	oír	to hear
		escribir	to write	olvidar	to forget
cerrar	to close	escuchar	to listen	parar(se)	to stop
coger	to take	esperar	to hope, wait for	parecer	to seem
comenzar	to start	estar resfriado	to have a cold	pasar la	to vacuum clean
comer	to eat	estar	to be	aspiradora	
comprar	to buy	faltar	to miss	pasar	to spend (time)
conducir	to drive	fumar	to smoke	pasear(se)	to go for a walk
conocer	to know (be familiar with)	ganar	to win, earn	patinar	to skate
		gastar	to spend (money)	pedir	to ask (for)
contestar	to answer, reply	golpear	to hit	pensar	to think
correr	to run	haber	to have (auxiliary verb)	perder	to lose
creer	to believe			poder	to be able to
cuidar	to look after	hablar	to speak	poner	to put
charlar	to chat	hacer	to do, make	poner la mesa	to lay the table
				preferir	to prefer
				preguntar	to ask (a question)

Now try this

Check your tenses by picking five verbs from each column and putting each one into the present, perfect and future tense for the first person (I) form.

① High frequency language

Verbs Q–V		Adjectives A–J		Adjectives L–V	
quedarse	to stay, remain	abierto/a	open	largo/a	long
quejarse	to complain	aburrido/a	boring	libre	free
querer	to like, want	activo/a	active	ligero/a	light
quitar la mesa	to clear the table	agradecido/a	grateful	limpio/a	clean
recordar	to remember	alegre	happy, cheerful	listo/a	ready
reembolsar	to refund	alto/a	high / tall	lleno/a	full
reír	to laugh	animado/a	lively	maduro/a	mature
rellenar (una ficha)	to fill out (a form)	antiguo/a	former, old	magnífico/a	magnificent
repasar	to revise	antipático/a	unpleasant	maravilloso/a	marvellous
robar	to steal	bello/a	beautiful	mismo/a	same
romper	to break	breve	brief	necesario/a	necessary
saber	to know (a fact)	brillante	brilliant	numeroso/a	numerous
sacar (buenas) notas	to get (good) marks	caliente	hot	otro/a	other
sacar entradas	to buy tickets	cansado/a	tired	pequeño/a	small
sacar fotos	to take photographs	castaño	chestnut brown	perdido/a	lost
salir	to leave	cercano/a	close	perezoso/a	lazy
saltar	to jump	cerrado/a	closed	perfecto/a	perfect
seguir	to follow, continue	cómodo/a	comfortable	pesado/a	heavy
sentarse	to sit down	corto/a	short	podrido/a	rotten
ser	to be	débil	weak	preferido/a	favourite
sonreír	to smile	delgado/a	thin	propio/a	own
subir	to climb, go up	difícil	difficult	próximo/a	next
tener	to have	divertido/a	amusing	rápido/a	fast, quick
tener calor / frío	to be hot / cold	duro/a	hard	responsable	responsible
tener éxito	to be successful	emocionante	exciting	rico/a	rich, delicious
tener hambre	to be hungry	enfadado/a	angry	roto/a	broken
tener prisa	to be in a hurry	estricto/a	strict	ruidoso/a	noisy
tener que	to have to	estupendo/a	great	sabio/a	wise
tener sed	to be thirsty	fácil	easy	sano/a	healthy
tener sueño	to be sleepy, tired	feo/a	ugly	satisfecho/a	satisfied
tener suerte	to be lucky	fuerte	strong	sensacional	sensational
tirar	to pull, throw	gordo/a	fat	serio/a	serious
tocar	to play (a musical instrument)	gran	great	severo/a	strict
tomar	to take	grande	big, tall	silencioso/a	silent
tomar el sol	to sunbathe	gratis	free	simpático/a	kind
torcer	to twist	guapo/a	handsome, pretty	solo/a	alone, lonely
trabajar	to work	guay	cool	sucio/a	dirty
traer	to bring	horrible	awful	tímido/a	shy
tratar de	to try to	igual	same	todo/a	all
triunfar	to succeed	ilusionado/a	excited	tonto/a	silly
utilizar	to use	increíble	unbelievable	trabajador(a)	hardworking
vender	to sell	joven	young	tradicional	traditional
venir	to come	junto/a	together	travieso/a	naughty
ver	to see			último/a	last, latest
vestirse	to get dressed			útil	useful
vivir	to live			válido/a	valid
				valiente	brave
				valioso/a	valuable
				verdadero/a	true
				viejo/a	old

Now try this

Choose 10 positive adjectives and 10 negative ones from this page. Write 10 sentences in Spanish using a different adjective in each.

① High frequency language

Adverbs

(por) mucho tiempo	(for a) long time
a menudo	often
a veces	sometimes
abajo	below (down)
afortunadamente	fortunately
ahí	over there
allí	there
aquí	here
arriba	up there
bastante	rather, quite
bien	well
casi	almost
demasiado	too
deprisa	quickly
desafortunadamente	unfortunately
enseguida	straight away
especialmente	especially
inmediatamente	immediately
mal	badly
más	more
muy	very
por todas partes	everywhere
quizás	perhaps
realmente	really
recientemente	recently
siempre	always
sobre todo	especially
todavía	still (yet)
ya	already

Connecting words

antes	before
aunque	though
después	then, afterwards
entonces	then
lo primero (de todo)	first of all
o / u	or
pero	but
pues	so
sin embargo	however
también	also
y / e	and

Time expressions

a partir de	from
a tiempo	on time
ahora	now
ahora mismo	just now, straight away

al comienzo	at the start
al día siguiente (m)	the next day
anoche	last night
anteayer	day before yesterday
año (m)	year
año pasado	last year
ayer	yesterday
cada día	everyday
de vez en cuando	from time to time
desde	since, from
día (m)	day
fin de semana (m)	weekend
hace	ago
hoy	today
luego	later
mañana	tomorrow
mañana (f)	morning
más tarde	later
medianoche (f)	midnight
minuto (m)	minute
noche (f)	night
pasado mañana	day after tomorrow
pasado/a	last
por la mañana	in the morning
por la noche	at night
por la tarde	in the afternoon
pronto	soon
próximo	next
puntual	on time
quince días	a fortnight
quincena (f)	a fortnight
semana (f)	week
siempre	always
siguiente	next
tarde (f)	next afternoon, evening
temprano	early
todos los días	everyday

Times

las dos y media

las tres menos cuarto

a la una	at one o'clock
a las dos	at two o'clock
a media noche	at midnight
a mediodía	at noon
de la mañana	in the morning
de la noche	at night
de la tarde	in the afternoon / evening
es la una	it's one o'clock
hora (f)	hour
menos cuarto	quarter to
menos diez, etc.	ten to, etc
minuto (m)	minute
son las dos, etc.	it's two o'clock, etc.
y cinco, etc.	five past, etc.
y cuarto	quarter past
y media	half past

Seasons

primavera (f)	spring
verano (m)	summer
otoño (m)	autumn
invierno (m)	winter

Colours

castaño	chestnut brown
claro/a	light
moreno/a	dark (hair, skin)
oscuro/a	dark
rubio/a	fair (hair, skin)
amarillo/a	
azul	
blanco/a	
gris	
marrón	
naranja	
negro/a	
rojo/a	
rosa	
verde	
violeta	

Now try this

Test yourself on the time expressions above by covering up the English column and then writing down the English translation yourself. Compare your answers with the list above. How many have you got right?

① High frequency language

Months of the year

enero	January
febrero	February
marzo	March
abril	April
mayo	May
junio	June
julio	July
agosto	August
septiembre	September
octubre	October
noviembre	November
diciembre	December

Quantities

bastante	enough
exactamente	exactly
mucho/a/s	much, many
nada	nothing
solamente	only
suficiente	enough
un kilo de	a kilo of
un litro de	a litre of
un paquete de	a packet of
un pedazo de	a piece of
un poco de	a little of
un tarro de	a jar of
un tercio de	a third of
una botella de	a bottle of
una caja de	a box of
una docena de	a dozen
una lata de	a tin of
una parte de	a part of
una rebanada de	a slice of
varios/as	several

Continents

África (f)	Africa
América del Norte (f)	North America
América del Sur (f)	South America
Asia (f)	Asia
Australia (f)	Australia
Europa (f)	Europe

lunes Monday	martes Tuesday	miércoles Wednesday	jueves Thursday	viernes Friday	sábado Saturday	domingo Sunday
07.00						
08.00						
09.00						
10.00						
11.00						
12.00						
13.00						
14.00						
15.00						
16.00						
17.00						
18.00						

Countries

Alemania (f)	
Austria (f)	Austria
Bélgica (f)	Belgium
Dinamarca (f)	Denmark
Escocia (f)	Scotland
España (f)	Spain
Estados Unidos (m/pl)	United States
Francia (f)	
Gran Bretaña (f)	
Grecia (f)	Greece
Holanda (f)	Holland
Inglaterra (f)	
Irlanda (f)	
Italia (f)	
Gales (m)	Wales
Países Bajos (m/pl)	Netherlands
Reino Unido (m)	United Kingdom
Rusia (f)	Russia
Suecia (f)	Sweden
Suiza (f)	

Nationalities

alemán/a	German
americano/a	American
austríaco/a	Austrian
belga	Belgian
británico/a	British
danés/esa	Danish
escocés/esa	Scottish
español/a	Spanish
europeo/a	European
francés/esa	French
galés/esa	Welsh
griego/a	Greek
holandés/esa	Dutch
inglés/esa	English
irlandés/esa	Irish
italiano/a	Italian
ruso/a	Russian
sueco/a	Swedish
suizo/a	Swiss

Now try this

Practise the days of the week and the months of the year by translating the birthdays of family and friends into Spanish.

① High frequency vocabulary

Prepositions

a	at, to
a causa de	because of
a través de	through
al final de	at the end of
al lado de	next to
alrededor de	about
antes	before
cerca de	near
con	with
contra	against
de, desde	from
debajo de	under
delante de	in front of
dentro (de)	inside
después	after
detrás	behind
durante	during
en	in, on
en casa de	at (someone's house)
en la esquina de	on the corner of
encima de	above
enfrente de	opposite
entre	between
excepto	except
fuera de	outside
hacia	towards
hasta	until
lejos (de)	far (from)
para	in order to, for
por	through, for
según	according to
sin	without
sobre	on

delante de   detrás de

al lado de   entre

cerca de   lejos de
near to   far from

Question words

¿Adónde? Where to?

¿Como? How?

¿Cuál? Which?

¿Cuántos/as? How many?

¿Dónde? Where?

¿Para qué? What for?

¿Cuándo? When?

¿Cuánto? How much?

¿Por qué? Why?

¿Qué? What?

¿Quien? Who?

Social conventions

¿Diga?	hello (on the telephone)
adiós	goodbye
buenas noches	goodnight
buenas tardes	good afternoon good evening
gracias	thank you
hasta luego	see you later
hasta mañana	see you tomorrow
hasta pronto	see you soon
hola	hi
buenos días	hello
muchas gracias	thank you very much
por favor	please
saludos	best wishes
¡Socorro!	Help!

Other useful expressions

¿Cómo se escribe?	How do you spell that?
aquí lo tienes	here you are
bien	OK
buena suerte	good luck
con (mucho) gusto	with pleasure
demasiado mal	too bad
depende	it depends
en mi opinión	in my opinion
estar a punto de	to be about to
Estoy bien.	I'm fine.
He tenido bastante.	I've had enough.
me da igual	I don't mind
mío/a	mine
no importa	it doesn't matter
normalmente	usually
otra vez	once again
qué pena	what a shame
por supuesto	of course

Now try this

Write a sentence in Spanish using each of the question words on this page.

108

2 Personal information

Friends and family

(no) gustar	to (dis)like
abuela (f)	grandmother
abuelito (m)	grandad
abuelo (m)	grandfather
abuelos (m/pl)	grandparents
agradable	likeable
alegre	cheerful
amigo/a (m/f)	friend
amistad (f)	friendship
anillo (m)	ring
animado/a	lively
anticuado/a	old-fashioned
antipático/a	unfriendly
año (m)	year
apellido (m)	surname
apodo (m)	nickname
apoyar	to support
atento/a	helpful
barba (f)	beard
bautizo (m)	christening
beso (m)	kiss
bigote (m)	moustache
boca (f)	mouth
boda (f)	wedding
bonito/a	pretty
cara (f)	face
casa (f)	house
casado/a	married
casarse	to get married
conocer	to know (be familiar with)
corresponsal (m/f)	penfriend
cuarto de baño (m)	bathroom
cuidar	to look after
cumpleaños (m)	birthday
chaqueta (f)	jacket
charlar	to chat
delgado/a	thin
desordenado/a	untidy
despacho (m)	study (room)
divertido/a	amusing
empleo (m)	job
en paro	unemployed
enfadado/a	angry
fecha de nacimiento (f)	date of birth
feo/a	ugly
gafas (f/pl)	glasses
gato (m)	cat

gemelos (m/pl)	twins
gente (f)	people
guapo/a	good-looking
hacer de canguro	to babysit
hermano (m)	brother
hermana (f)	sister
lindo/a	pretty
llevarse bien con	to get on with
madre (f)	mother
molestar	to annoy
muelas (f/pl)	teeth
nariz (f)	nose
ojos (m/pl)	eyes
ordenador (m)	computer
padre (m)	father
padres (m/pl)	parents
pasado/a de moda	out of date
pelear	to quarrel
pendientes (m/pl)	earrings
perro (m)	dog
piso (m)	flat
rizado/a	curly
ropa (f)	clothes
sueño (m)	dream
tía (f)	aunt
tío (m)	uncle
triste	sad
vecino/a (m/f)	neighbour
vida (f)	life

H (Higher)

apagar	to switch off
bien equilibrado/a	well-balanced
calvo/a	bald
carrera (f)	career
celoso/a	jealous
deprimido/a	depressed
jubilado/a	retired
loco/a	crazy
necesitado/a	needy
nieto/a (m/f)	grandson/-daughter
novio/a (m/f)	bride/-groom, fiancé(e), boy/girlfriend
parecido/a	similar
pariente (m/f)	relative
sin hogar	homeless
sobrino/a (m/f)	nephew / niece

Leisure activities

actividad (f)	activity
ajedrez (m)	chess
atletismo (m)	athletics
bailar	to dance
balón de fútbol (m)	football
baloncesto (m)	basketball
barbacoa (f)	barbecue
batería	drums, percussion
bolera (f)	bowling alley
campeonato (m)	championship
campo deportivo (m)	sportsground
ciclismo (m)	cycling
cine (m)	cinema
clásico/a	classical, classic
club juvenil (m)	youth club
chándal (m)	tracksuit
dar un paseo	to go for a stroll
descansar	to rest
discoteca (f)	disco
diversión (f)	fun
encontrar	to meet, to find
entrada (f)	(entrance) ticket, entry
equipo (m)	team
equipo de deportes (m)	sports equipment
equitación (f)	horse-riding
esquí (acuático) (m)	(water) skiing
fútbol (m)	football
gol (m)	goal (scored in football)
grupo (m)	band, group
hacer deporte	to do sport
hacer ejercicio	to exercise
hacer gimnasia	to do gymnastics
lanzar	to bowl
meta (f)	goal
montar en monopatín	to skateboard
música (f)	music
nadar	to swim
natación (f)	swimming
obra de teatro (f)	play (theatre)
ocio (m)	leisure activity
ofrecer	to offer
orquesta (f)	orchestra
pasatiempo (m)	hobby

Now try this

To help you learn the personality adjectives, write out the Spanish adjectives on this page in three lists: positive, negative and neutral. Then memorise five adjectives that could describe you.

② Personal information

pescar	to fish
piscina al aire libre (f)	open-air swimming pool
piscina cubierta (f)	indoor swimming pool
plaza de toros (f)	bull ring
practicar la vela	to sail
precio de entrada (m)	entrance fee
salir	to go out
sesión (f)	performance
tenis (de mesa) (m)	(table) tennis
tirar	to shoot
barco de vela (m)	sailing boat
videojuego (m)	computer game
zapatillas de deporte (f/pl)	trainers

HIGHER H

aceptar	to accept
alpinismo (m)	mountaineering
practicar el buceo	to scuba dive
caña de pesca (f)	fishing rod
deporte (m)	sport
escalada en rocas (f)	rock-climbing
lanzar en paracaídas	parachuting
tirarse (al agua)	to dive
tiro con arco (m)	archery

Lifestyle: healthy eating and exercise

FOUNDATION Fn

accidente (m)	accident
aceite (m)	oil
agua (f)	water
agua mineral (f) (con gas, sin gas)	mineral water (fizzy, still)
albaricoque (m)	apricot
almuerzo (m)	lunch
arroz (m)	rice

Toco ...   I play ...

violín (m)   guitarra (f)   trompeta (f)   flauta (f)

clarinete (m)   piano (m)   banjo (m)   batería (f)

flauta dulce (f)   arpa (f)   saxofón (m)   pandereta (f)

asado (m)	roast
atún (m)	tuna
azúcar (m/f)	sugar
beber	to drink
bocadillo (m)	sandwich
brazo (m)	arm
cabeza (f)	head
cacao (m)	cocoa
caer	to fall
cansado/a	tired
caramelos (m/pl)	sweets
carne (f)	meat
carne de cerdo (f)	pork
cebolla (f)	onion
cena (f)	evening meal
ciclismo (m)	cycling
ciruela (f)	plum
coliflor (f)	cauliflower

comer	to eat
comida (f)	meal, food, lunch
corazón (m)	heart
correr	to run
crema (f)	cream
crudo/a	raw
cuerpo (m)	body
champiñón (m)	mushroom
chuleta (f)	chop
dedo (m)	finger
dejar de	to give up
delgado/a	slim
deporte (m)	sport
deportista (m/f)	sportsman/woman
desayunar	to have breakfast
desayuno (m)	breakfast

Now try this

To help you learn the leisure activities vocabulary, make a list of five activities that you like doing and five that you don't like doing then memorise them.

② Personal information

diente (m)	tooth	melón (m)	melon	terapia (f)	therapy
dolor (m)	pain	mermelada (f)	jam	tomar (medicina)	to take (medicine)
dormir	to sleep	naranja (f)	orange	tomate (m)	tomato
dulce	sweet	naranjada (f)	orangeade	tortilla (f)	omelette
duro/a	hard	nata (f)	cream	tostada (f)	toast
enfermo/a	ill	orgánico/a	organic	uva (f)	grape
ensalada (f)	salad	pan (m)	bread	verduras (f/pl)	vegetables
espalda (f)	back (part of body)	panecillo (m)	roll	viejo/a	old
		pastel (m)	cake	vino (tinto, blanco) (m)	wine (red, white)
estómago (m)	stomach	patata (f)	potato		
feliz	happy	patatas fritas (f/pl)	chips, crisps	vitaminas (f/pl)	vitamins
frambuesa (f)	raspberry			yogur (m)	yoghurt
fresa (f)	strawberry	pepino (m)	cucumber	zanahoria (f)	carrot
fruta (f)	fruit	pera (f)	pear	zumo (de fruta) (m)	(fruit) juice
fumar	to smoke	perder peso	to lose weight		
galleta (f)	biscuit	pescado (m)	fish		
ganar peso	to put on weight	picante	hot (spicy)		
garganta (f)	neck, throat	pie (m)	foot		
golosinas (f/pl)	sweets	pierna (f)	leg		
gordo/a	fat	piña (f)	pineapple	acostumbrarse a	to get used to
grasa (f)	fat, grease	plátano (m)	banana	ajo (m)	garlic
grasiento/a	fatty, greasy	pollo (m)	chicken	alimentación (f)	food
gripe (m)	flu	postre (m)	dessert	asar	to roast
guisante (m)	pea	preparar	to prepare	carne de cordero (f)	lamb
hacer ejercicio	to exercise	probar	to try		
hacer footing	to jog	pulmón (m)	lung	carne de vaca (f)	beef
hambre (f)	hunger	queso (m)	cheese	engordar	to put on weight
helado (m)	ice cream	receta (f)	recipe	freír	to fry
herida (f)	injury	relajarse	to relax	harina (f)	flour
hombro (m)	shoulder	riquísimo/a	delicious	huevo frito (m)	fried egg
huevo (m)	egg	rodilla (f)	knee	huevos revueltos (m/pl)	scrambled eggs
intentar	to try to	romper	to break		
jamón (serrano, de York) (m)	ham (cured, cooked)	roto/a	broken	leche entera (f)	full fat milk
		sabroso/a	tasty	merluza (f)	hake
judía (f)	bean	sal (f)	salt	miel (f)	honey
leche (f)	milk	salchicha (f)	sausage	muy hecho	well-cooked
lechuga (f)	lettuce	salud (f)	health	nuez (f)	nut
limón (m)	lemon	sopa (f)	soup	obesidad (f)	obesity
limonada (f)	lemonade	tarta (f)	tart, cake	olor (m)	smell
lleno/a	full	té (m)	tea	pato (m)	duck
malo/a	bad	temperatura (f)	temperature	pavo (m)	turkey
mano (f)	hand	tener dolor de ...	to have ...-ache	quemadura (f)	burn
mantenerse en forma	to keep fit	tener hambre	to be hungry	resfriado (m)	cold
		tener miedo	to be afraid	sabor (m)	taste
manzana (f)	apple	tener sed	to be thirsty	sazonar	to season
me duele el/la ...	my ... hurts	tener tos	to have a cough	ternera (f)	veal
melocotón (m)	peach			trucha (f)	trout

Now try this

Write at least 10 body parts in Spanish from memory. Look at the page and check your spelling.

③ Out and about

Visitor information

F FOUNDATION

¡Que lo pases bien!	Enjoy your stay!
abierto/a	open
acera (f)	pavement
afueras (f/pl)	outskirts
al aire libre	in the open air
al extranjero	abroad
aldea (f)	village
alquiler de coches / bicicletas (m)	car / bike hire
apartamento (m)	apartment
autopista (f)	motorway
barrio (m)	part of town
basura (f)	rubbish
bienvenido/a	welcome
bosque (m)	wood
café (m)	café
campo (m)	field, countryside
capital (f)	capital city
carnet de identidad (m)	identity card
castillo (m)	castle
catedral (f)	cathedral
cerrado/a	closed
cerveza de barril (f)	draught beer
cita (f)	appointment
ciudad (f)	city
colina (f)	hill
concierto (m)	concert
contaminación (f)	pollution
control de pasaportes (m)	passport control
costa (f)	coast
entretenimiento (m)	entertainment
excursión (f)	tour
exposición (f)	exhibition
fiesta (f)	festival
fiesta nacional (f)	public holiday
folleto (m)	brochure / leaflet
función (f)	performance
habitante (m/f)	inhabitant
histórico/a	historic

horas de apertura (f/pl)	opening hours
información turística (f)	tourist information
isla (f)	island
lago (m)	lake
lista de precios (f)	price list
lugar de interés (m)	place of interest
mapa de carreteras (m)	road map
mar (m)	sea
mercado (m)	market
montaña (f)	mountain
naturaleza (f)	nature
ocio (m)	leisure
oficina de turismo (f)	tourist information office
país (m)	country
parque de atracciones (m)	amusement park
parque zoológico (m)	zoo
película (f)	film
pintoresco/a	picturesque
piso (m)	flat
plano (m)	map
playa (f)	beach
plaza (f)	square
polución (f)	pollution
postal (f)	postcard
precio de entrada (m)	entry fee
prohibido/a	forbidden
pueblo (m)	town
reducción (f)	reduction
región (f)	region
reservar	to book
río (m)	river

robo (m)	theft
salida (f)	exit
selva (f)	forest
señal (f)	sign
sitio (m)	place
tarjeta telefónica (f)	telephone card
torre (f)	tower
tranquilo/a	quiet
turista (m/f)	tourist
vale la pena ver	well worth seeing
vida nocturna (f)	nightlife
zona (f)	part of town
zona peatonal (f)	pedestrian area
zona residencial (f)	suburb

H HIGHER

aduana (f)	customs
aire acondicionado (m)	air conditioning
alrededores (m/pl)	surrounding area
desfile (m)	procession
estancia (f)	stay
fuegos artificiales (m/pl)	fireworks
fuente (f)	fountain
hospitalidad (f)	hospitality
rastro (m)	fleamarket
recuerdo (m)	souvenir
salida de emergencia (f)	emergency exit
suceso (m)	event
tener lugar	to take place
zona verde (f)	park, green space

al / en el norte
in the north

al / en el oeste
in the west

al / en el este
in the east

al / en el sur
in the south

Now try this

Pick out 10–15 words from this page that you could use to describe a recent trip or holiday. memorise them, then try to write a short sentence with each.

③ Out and about

Weather

boletín meteorológico (m)	weather report
brillar	to shine
buen tiempo (m)	good weather
calor (m)	heat
caluroso/a	hot
cambiar	to change
cielo (m)	sky
clima (m)	climate
helada (f)	frost
viento (m)	wind
está nublado	it's overcast
frío	cold
grado (m)	degree (temperature)
hace mucho frío	it's freezing
hay niebla	it's foggy
hay relámpagos	there's lightning
hay truenos	there's thunder
llover	to rain
llueve, está lloviendo	it's raining
lluvia (f)	rain
lluvioso/a	rainy
mal tiempo (m)	bad weather
nieva, está nevando	it is snowing
nieve (f)	snow
nube (f)	cloud
seco/a	dry
sol (m)	sun
soleado/a	sunny
temperatura más alta (f)	highest temperature
tiempo (m)	weather
tormenta (f)	storm
viento (m)	wind

alto/a	high
bajo/a	low
despejarse	to brighten up
granizo (m)	hail
medio/a	average
período soleado (m)	bright spell
precipitación (f)	rainfall
pronóstico meteorológico (m)	weather forecast

tormentoso/a	stormy
variable	changeable

Local amenities

abierto/a	open
aeropuerto (m)	airport
aseos (m/pl)	toilets
ayuntamiento (m)	town hall
banco (m)	bank
biblioteca (f)	library
bloque de pisos (m)	tower block
bolera (f)	bowling alley (10-pin)
café (m)	café
cafetería (f)	snack bar
castillo (m)	castle
cathedral (f)	cathedral
centro comercial (m)	shopping centre
cerrado/a	closed
cine (m)	cinema
club nocturno (m)	nightclub
comercio (m)	business
comisaría (f)	police station
discoteca (f)	disco
edificio (m)	building
estación de autobuses (f)	bus station
estación de ferrocarril (f)	railway station
estadio (m)	stadium
fábrica (f)	factory
gasolinera (f)	petrol station
granja (f)	farm
hospital (m)	hospital
iglesia (f)	church
industria (f)	industry
lavandería (automática) (f)	laundry (launderette)
mercado (m)	market
municipal	public, municipal
museo (m)	museum
negocio (m)	business
oficina de correos (f)	post office
palacio (m)	palace
parque (m)	park
patio (de recreo) (m)	playground
pista de patinaje (sobre hielo) (f)	ice rink
plaza (f)	square
policía (m/f)	police officer

polideportivo (m)	leisure centre
puente (m)	bridge
puerto (m)	port
quiosco (m)	newspaper stall
servicios (m/pl)	toilets
teatro (m)	theatre
tienda (f)	shop
wáter (m)	WC

caja de ahorros (f)	savings bank
cajero automático (m)	cashpoint, ATM
cancha de tenis (f)	tennis court
cubo de basura (m)	rubbish bin
torre de pisos (m)	tower block
zona peatonal (f)	pedestrian area

Accommodation

acampar	to camp
agua potable (f)	drinking water
albergue juvenil (m)	youth hostel
aldea (f)	village
alojamiento (m)	accommodation
alquería (f)	farm house
alquilar	to hire, rent
amueblado/a	furnished
armario (m)	wardrobe
ascensor (m)	lift
balcón (m)	balcony
bañera (f)	bath tub
calefacción (f)	heating
cama (f)	bed
camping (m)	campsite
caravana (f)	caravan
cocina (f)	kitchen
comedor (m)	dining area
cuarto de baño (m)	bathroom
cuarto de estar (m)	living room
dar a	to overlook
deshacer la maleta	to unpack
dormitorio (m)	bedroom
ducha (f)	shower
en el campo	in the country
en el primer piso	on the 1st floor
equipaje (m)	luggage

Now try this

Without looking at the book, think of your local town or city and write a list of all of the amenities that it has in Spanish..

③ Out and about

escalera (f)	staircase	barato/a	cheap	permiso de conducir (m)	driving licence
ficha (f)	form	normas de la casa (f/pl)	rules of the house	puerta (f)	door
habitación doble (f)	double room	ruido (m)	noise	puerto (m)	port
habitación individual (f)	single room	salida de emergencia (f)	emergency exit	reducción (f)	reduction
huésped (m/f)	guest			retraso (m)	delay
jabón (m)	soap			revisor(a) (m/f) inspector	ticket inspector
jardín (m)	garden			rotonda (f)	roundabout
lavabo (m)	wash basin			sala de espera (f)	waiting room
libre	vacant			salida (f)	departure, exit

Public transport

litera (f)	bunk bed	aeropuerto (m)	airport	semáforos (m/pl)	traffic lights
llave (f)	key	andén (m)	platform	señal (f)	sign
llegada (f)	arrival	aparcamiento (m)	car park	sin plomo	unleaded
maleta (f)	suitcase	asiento (m)	seat	tardar	to be delayed, to be late
media pensión (f)	half-board	atasco (m)	traffic jam		
ocupado/a	occupied	aterrizar	to land	tranvía (f)	tram
pasar la noche	to spend the night	autobús (m)	bus	tren (m)	train
		autocar (m)	coach	vía (f)	platform, track
pensión (f)	guest house	autopista (f)	motorway	viaje (m)	journey
pensión completa (f)	full board	avería (f)	breakdown		
		avión (m)	plane		
piso (m)	floor, flat	barco (m)	boat		
planta (f)	floor	bici (f)	bike	abrochar	to fasten
planta baja (f)	ground floor	billete (m)	ticket	adelantar	to overtake
puerta (principal) (f)	door (front)	camión (m)	lorry	apresurarse	to hurry
		carretera (f)	road	área de servicios (f)	picnic area
ropa de cama (f)	bed linen	carril de bicicleta (m)	cycle path	cinturón de seguridad (m)	seatbelt
saco de dormir (m)	sleeping bag	ciclomotor (m)	moped		
sala de estar (f)	living room	circulación (f)	traffic	frenar	to brake
sala de juegos (f)	games room	coche (m)	car	hora punta (f)	rush hour
		consigna (f)	left luggage	límite de velocidad (m)	speed limit
salida (f)	exit	convalidar	to validate a ticket		
salón (m)	lounge				

Directions

segundo/a	second	de ida	single		
sótano (m)	basement	de ida y vuelta	return		
suelo (m)	floor	de segunda clase	second class		
tienda (f)	tent	despacho de billetes (m)	ticket office	a la izquierda	on the left
toalla de baño (f)	bath towel			a la derecha	on the right
ventana (f)	window	despegar	to take off (plane)	cruzar	to cross
vista (f)	view	desvío (m)	detour	perdone	excuse me
		enlace (m)	connection	todo recto	straight on
		gasoil (m)	diesel		
aire acondicionado (m)	air conditioning	gasolina (f)	petrol		
		horario (m)	timetable		
alojamiento (m)	board and lodgings	máquina de billetes (f)	ticket machine		
alojarse	to stay	parada (f)	bus stop	cruce (m)	crossroads
apagar	to switch off	paso de peatones (m)	pedestrian crossing	esquina (f)	corner
				estar situado/a	to be situated
				lejos	far

Now try this

Imagine travelling from your home town to Madrid. Describe in Spanish all the forms of transport you might need.

4 Customer service and transactions

Cafés and restaurants

¡Que aproveche!	Enjoy your meal!
aceite de oliva (m)	olive oil
aceituna (f)	olive
albóndiga (f)	meatball
apetito (m)	appetite
asado/a	roast(ed)
café (m)	coffee
camarero/a (m/f)	waiter / waitress
carta (f)	menu
cereza (f)	cherry
cerveza (f)	beer
cliente (m/f)	customer
cocinado/a	cooked
col (f)	cabbage
col de Bruselas (f)	Brussels sprout
comedor (m)	dining room
copa (f)	glass
crema (f)	cream
cubiertos (m/pl)	cutlery
cuchara (f)	spoon
cucharilla (f)	teaspoon
cuchillo (m)	knife
cuenta (f)	bill
chocolate (m)	chocolate
churros (m/pl)	fritters
autoservicio (m)	self-service
día de descanso (m)	day off
dinero (m)	money
embutidos (m/pl)	cold sliced meat
entrada (f)	starter
especialidad (f)	speciality
flan (m)	caramel custard
guisado (m)	stew
haba (f)	bean
hamburguesa (f)	hamburger
heladería (f)	ice cream parlour
hervido/a	boiled
loza (f)	crockery
mantel (m)	tablecloth
menú del día (m)	set meal

zanahoria (f)   seta (f)   cebolla (f)   guisante (m)

pimiento (m)   patata (f)   tomate (m)   pepino (m)

mesa (f)	table
mezclado/a	mixed
mostaza (f)	mustard
opción (f)	choice
pagar	to pay
perrito caliente (m)	hot dog
pincho (m)	kebab
plato del día (m)	dish of the day
plato principal (m)	main course
propina (f)	tip (money)
queja (f)	complaint
ración (f)	portion
refrescos (m/pl)	refreshments
salsa (f)	gravy, sauce
sandía (f)	watermelon
servicio (m)	service
servilleta (f)	napkin
servir	to serve
taberna (f)	inn
tarjeta de crédito (f)	credit card
taza (f)	cup
té (m)	tea
tenedor (m)	fork
tentempié (m)	snack
terraza (f)	terrace

torta (f)	cake, tart
vainilla (f)	vanilla
vajilla (f)	crockery
vaso (m)	glass
vinagre (m)	vinegar

ahumado/a	smoked
bandeja (f)	tray
calamares (m/pl)	squid
casero/a	homemade
cereales (m/pl)	cereals
champán (m)	champagne
espinacas (f/pl)	spinach
gambas (f/pl)	prawns
ganso (m)	goose
leche (desnatada) (f)	(skimmed) milk
lomo (de cerdo) (m)	loin (of pork)
mariscos (m/pl)	seafood
mejillones (m/pl)	mussels
merienda (f)	afternoon snack
muy hecho	well-cooked
platillo (m)	saucer
tazón (m)	mug

Now try this

Think about what you have eaten and drunk today. Check that you can say it all and write it out correctly in Spanish.

4 Customer service and transactions

Shops

calcetín (m)

cinturón (m)

bufanda (f)

zapato (m)

sombrero (m)

corbata (f)

abanico (m)	fan
abrigo (m)	coat
agotado/a	sold out
algodón (m)	cotton
ascensor (m)	lift
banco (m)	bank
bañador (m)	swimming costume
barato/a	cheap
bebida (f)	drink
billete de banco (m)	bank note
billete de diez libras esterlinas (m)	a £10 note
billetera (f)	wallet
blusa (f)	blouse
bolsa de la compra (f)	shopping bag
bolso de mano (m)	handbag
botas (f/pl)	boots
bragas (f/pl)	pants, briefs
caja (f)	till, check-out
caja de cambio (f)	bureau de change
calidad (f)	quality
calzoncillos (m/pl)	underpants
calzones (m/pl)	boxers
cámara fotográfica (f)	camera
cambio (m)	change (i.e. coins)
camisa (f)	shirt
camiseta (f)	T-shirt
camisón de noche (m)	nightdress
cantidad (f)	quantity
carnicería (f)	butcher's
caro/a	expensive
carrito de la compra (m)	shopping trolley
céntimo (m)	cent
centrocomercial (m)	shopping centre
cepillo (m)	brush

cesta (f)	shopping basket
chándal (m)	tracksuit
chaqueta (f)	jacket
cheque de viaje (m)	(traveller's) cheque
chicle (m)	chewing gum
collar (m)	necklace
compras (f/pl)	shopping
crema de sol (f)	suncream
de cuadros	checked
de rayas	striped
dependiente/a (m/f)	sales assistant
droguería (f)	chemist's
económico/a	low priced
efectivo (m)	cash
entregar	to deliver
escalera mecánica (f)	escalator
escaparate (m)	shop window
estanco (m)	tobacconist's
falda (f)	skirt
farmacia (f)	pharmacy
ferretería (f)	hardware shop
fiambres (m/pl)	cold meats
flor (f)	flower
floristería (f)	florist's
folleto (m)	brochure
frágil	fragile
gastar (dinero)	to spend (money)
gorra (f)	cap
grandes almacenes (m/pl)	department store
gratis	free of charge

guante (m)	glove
hacer cola	to queue
hacer la maleta	to pack
hipermercado (m)	hypermarket
horas de apertura (f/pl)	opening hours
impermeable (m)	raincoat
ir bien	to suit
ir de compras	to go shopping
jarabe (m)	syrup
jersey (m)	jumper
joyas (f/pl)	jewellery
joyería (f)	jeweller's
lana (f)	wool
libra (f)	pound (weight, sterling)
librería (f)	bookshop
lista (f)	list
lista de la compra (f)	shopping list
mantequilla (f)	butter
marca (f)	make, brand
medias (f/pl)	tights
mercado (m)	market
moda (f)	fashion
moneda (f)	coin
monedero (m)	purse
muñeca (f)	doll
número (m)	size (shoes)
oferta de ocasión (f)	special offer
opción (f)	choice
pagar	to pay
panadería (f)	baker's

Now try this

Look at the clothes that you and your friends are wearing today. Check that you can translate them all into Spanish and spell them correctly.

④ Customer service and transactions

pantalón (m)	trousers	tienda (f)	shop	comisaría (f)	police station
papelería (f)	stationer's	tienda de comestibles (f)	grocer's	cuenta bancaria (f)	bank account
paraguas (m)	umbrella				
pastelería (f)	cake shop	tienda de ropa (f)	clothes shop	daño (m)	damage
patrón (m)	boss			dinero (m)	money
peine (m)	comb	toalla (f)	towel	enfermedad (f)	illness
peluquería (f)	hairdresser	traje (m)	suit	enfermo/a	ill
pendiente (m)	earring	traje de baño (m)	swimming costume	error (m)	mistake
perfume (m)	perfume			euro (m)	euro
perfumería (f)	perfumery	venta (f)	sale	ficha (f)	form
pescadería (f)	fishmonger's	vendedor/a (m/f)	salesman / saleswoman	formulario (m)	form
piel (f)	leather			guardar	to keep
precio (m)	price	verdulería (f)	greengrocer's	hospital (m)	hospital
prensa (f)	press	vestido (m)	dress	jefe (m/f)	boss
probarse	to try on	vestuario (m)	changing room	ladrón/ona (m/f)	thief
quedar bien	to fit	vuelo (m)	flight	oficina de objetos perdidos (f)	lost property office
quiosco (m)	(newspaper) kiosk	zapatería (f)	shoe shop		
		zapatilla (f)	slipper		
rebaja (f)	reduction	zapatillas de deporte (f/pl)	trainers	perder	to lose
rebajas (f/pl)	sales			plano de la ciudad (m)	town map
recibo (m)	receipt				
recuerdo (m)	souvenir			problema (m)	problem
reducción (f)	reduction			quejarse	to complain
reducido/a	reduced	albornoz (m)	bathrobe	recibir un reembolso	to get one's money back
regalo (m)	present	bata (f)	dressing gown		
repartir	to deliver post	cambiar un cheque	to cash a cheque	recibo (m)	receipt
ropa (f)	clothes			reloj (m)	clock, watch
salida de emergencia (f)	emergency exit	rebeca (f)	cardigan	robo (m)	theft
		charcutería (f)	delicatessen	roto/a	broken
sandalia (f)	sandal	envase (m)	packaging	ruido (m)	noise
sección (f)	department	etiqueta (f)	label	servicio de atención al cliente (m)	customer service
sello (m)	stamp	fecha de consumo preferente (f)	best-before date		
servicio (m)	service				
sostén (m)	bra			taquilla (f)	ticket office
suéter (m)	sweater	liquidación (f)	(clearance) sale	tipo de cambio (m)	exchange rate
supermercado (m)	supermarket	plástico (m)	plastic		
surtido (m)	choice, selection	rebajado/a	reduced	tos (f)	cough
tabaco (m)	tobacco	seda (f)	silk	verdad (f)	truth
talla (f)	size (clothes)	tienda de muebles (f)	furniture shop		
tarjeta bancaria (f)	bank card				

Dealing with problems

tarjeta de crédito (f)	credit card		asegurar	to insure
té (m)	tea		cárcel (f)	prison
te / le va bien	it fits / suits you		dañar	to damage
te / le queda bien	it fits / suits you	ambulancia (f)	ambulance	demostrar	to prove
teclado (m)	keyboard	avería (f)	breakdown	desaparecer	to disappear
tendero/a (m/f)	shopkeeper	cambio (m)	change	probar	to prove
		carnet de identidad (m)	identity card	seguro (m)	insurance
				tratar con	to deal with

Now try this

Use this page and the previous one to list 10 types of shop in Spanish and then list two items that you buy in each shop.

⑤ Future plans, education and work

Basic language of the internet

Fn (FOUNDATION)

archivar	to save
borrar	to erase
chat (m)	chatroom
chatear	to chat (online)
contraseña (de acceso) (f)	password
correo electrónico (m)	email
descargar	to download
enlace (m)	connection
escribir a ordenador	to type
impresora (f)	printer
imprimir	to print
ordenador (m)	computer
página de Internet (f)	internet page
página de inicio (f)	homepage
página web (f)	webpage
pantalla (f)	screen
programador (a) (m/f)	programmer
quemar	to burn
ratón (m)	mouse
software (m)	software
sondeo (m)	survey
subir	to upload
tecla (f)	key (of keyboard)
virus (m)	virus
web site (m)	website

H (HIGHER)

arroba (f)	@ (in email address)
archivo de datos (m)	(data) file
mundial	worldwide
raya baja (f)	underscore

Simple job advertisements

Fn (FOUNDATION)

actor (m)	actor
agricultor(a) (m/f)	farmer
albañil (m/f)	builder
anuncio (m)	advert
arquitecto/a (m/f)	architect
auxiliar de vuelo (m/f)	cabin attendant
azafata (f)	air hostess
bombero/a (m/f)	firefighter
carnicero/a (m/f)	butcher
carta (f)	letter
cocinero/a (m/f)	cook
compañía (f)	company
dentista (m/f)	dentist
diseñador(a) (m/f)	designer
diseño (m)	design
electricista (m/f)	electrician
empleo (m)	job
empresa (f)	company
enfermero/a (m/f)	nurse
entrevista (f)	interview
experiencia laboral (f)	work experience
fontanero/a (m/f)	plumber
formación (f)	training
funcionario/a (m/f)	civil servant
futbolista (m/f)	footballer
horas de trabajo (f/pl)	hours of work
informático/a (m/f)	computer scientist
ingeniero/a (m/f)	engineer
mecánico/a (m/f)	mechanic
médico/a (m/f)	doctor
medios de comunicación (m/pl)	media
modelo (m/f)	model
ofertas de empleo (f/pl)	situations vacant
panadero/a (m/f)	baker
periodista (m/f)	journalist
por hora	per hour
programador(a) (m/f)	programmer

rellenar (una ficha)	to fill in (a form)
solicitud (f)	application
taxista (m/f)	taxi driver
técnico/a (m/f)	technician

H (HIGHER)

| posibilidades de ascenso (f/pl) | promotion prospects |

Simple job applications and CV

Fn (FOUNDATION)

adjunto/a	enclosed
al año próximo	next year
anuncio de trabajo (m)	job advert
aprendizaje (m)	apprenticeship
boletín escolar (m)	school report
C.V. (m)	CV
carta (f)	letter
con experiencia	experienced
educación escolar (f)	school education
entrevista (f)	interview
firma (f)	signature
formación (f)	training
presentarse	to introduce oneself
profesión (f)	profession
puesto (m)	position
remitir	to send
solicitar un empleo	to apply for a job
tener éxito	to be successful
titulado/a	qualified
título (m)	qualification
universidad (f)	university

H (HIGHER)

carta de solicitud (f)	letter of application
entrevista para un empleo (f)	job interview
ficha de solicitud (f)	application form

Now try this

To help you learn the jobs vocabulary, make a list of five jobs that you would like to do and five jobs that you would not like to do and then memorise them.

⑤ Future plans, education and work

Work and work experience

a tiempo completo	full-time
a tiempo parcial	part-time
agencia de viajes (f)	travel agency
amo/a de casa (m/f)	housewife/-husband
bien pagado/a	well paid
buzón (m)	letter box
cajero/a (m/f)	cashier
camarero/a (m/f)	waiter, waitress
camionero/a (m/f)	lorry driver
carpintero/a (m/f)	joiner, carpenter
carrera (f)	career
cartero/a (m/f)	postman/-woman
cocinero/a (m/f)	cook
colega (m/f)	colleague
comedor (m)	canteen
condiciones de empleo (f/pl)	terms of employment
conductor(a) (m/f)	driver
construir	to build
contestador (automático) (m)	answerphone
dentista (m/f)	dentist
dependiente/a (m/f)	sales assistant
despedir	to fire
dueño/a (m/f)	owner
fábrica (f)	factory
farmacéutico/a (m/f)	chemist
feria comercial (f)	trade fair
florista (m/f)	florist
gerente (m/f)	manager
granjero/a (m/f)	farmer
guía telefónica (f)	telephone directory, telephone book
hacer trabajo eventual	to do casual work

hombre / mujer de negocios (m/f)	businessman/-woman
hora del almuerzo (f)	lunch break
horas de trabajo (f/pl)	hours of work, working hours
huelga (f)	strike
impresión (f)	impression
independiente	independent
jardinero/a (m/f)	gardener
jefe/a (m/f)	boss
llamada telefónica (f)	telephone call
mal pagado/a	badly paid
marketing (m)	marketing
médico/a (m/f)	doctor
mensaje (m)	message
nombrar	to appoint, to take on
objetivo (m)	aim
obrero/a (m/f)	worker
ocupado/a	busy
oficina (f)	office
oportunidad (f)	opportunity
paga (f)	pay
papel (m)	paper
pintor(a) (m/f)	painter
planeado/a	planned
ponerse de pie	to stand
por hora	per hour
poseer	to own
preocupación (f)	worry
presentarse	to introduce oneself
programador(a) de ordenadores (m/f)	computer programmer
secretario/a (m/f)	secretary
sello (m)	stamp
sobre (m)	envelope
soldado (m/f)	soldier
sueldo (m)	salary
taller (m)	workshop
telefonear	to phone
teléfono móvil (m)	mobile phone
tolerar	to put up with
trabajar	to work
trabajar desde casa	to work from home
veterinario/a (m/f)	vet
volver a llamar	to call back

HIGHER

abogado/a (m/f)	lawyer
aprendiz(a) (m/f)	trainee
aspirante (m/f)	applicant
autor(a) (m/f),	author
candidato/a (m/f)	candidate
cinta transportadora (f)	conveyor belt
comerciante (m/f)	retailer
contable (m/f)	accountant
decidir	to decide
derecho (m)	law
despedir	to dismiss
dimitir	to resign
discusión (f)	discussion
escritor(a) (m/f)	writer
estar de acuerdo con	to agree on
formación profesional (f)	professional training
para desempleados (m)	for the unemployed
horario flexible (m)	flexitime
igualdad (f)	equality
intérprete (m/f)	interpreter
oficina de empleo (f)	job centre
poner con	to put someone through (on telephone)
renunciar	to hand in notice
reunión (f)	meeting
tarea (f)	task
trabajo eventual	casual work
trabajo por turnos (m)	shift work
voluntario/a (m/f)	volunteer

Now try this

Think of a work experience that you have done or would like to do and list 10–15 words on this page that might apply to it. Learn them, then write or say them from memory. As an extra challenge, try to write a sentence with each of them.

⑤ Future plans, education and work

School and college

adecuado/a	satisfactory
alemán (m)	German
alumno/a (m/f)	pupil
asignatura (f)	subject
aula (f)	classroom
bachillerato (m)	equivalent of GCE A levels
biblioteca (f)	library
biología (f)	biology
bolígrafo (m), boli	ballpoint pen
calculadora (f)	calculator
campo deportivo (m)	sports field
cantina (f)	canteen
ciclomotor (m)	moped
ciencias (f/pl)	sciences
ciencias de la información (f/pl)	media studies
consejero/a de orientación profesional (m/f)	careers adviser
consejo de estudiantes (m)	student council
coro (m)	choir
corregir	to correct
deberes (m/pl)	homework
débil	unsatisfactory
dibujo (m)	art
diccionario (m)	dictionary
director(a) (m/f)	headteacher
diseño (m)	DT
educación física (f)	PE
Educación Secundaria Obligatoria (f)	GCSE equivalent
enseñanza religiosa (f)	Religious Studies
equipo (m)	team
escrito/a	written
escritorio (m)	desk
escuela de formación profesional (f)	vocational school
escuela infantil (f)	nursery school
escuela primaria (f)	primary school
escuela privada (f)	private school
español (m)	Spanish
estado (m)	state

estuche (m)	pencil case
estudiante (m/f)	student
estudiar	to study
examen (m)	examination
excursión organizada por el colegio (f)	school trip
física (f)	physics
francés (m)	French
fuerte	good at (subject)
geografía (f)	geography
gimnasio (m)	gym
goma (f)	rubber
historia (f)	history
hora de la comida (f)	lunch break
idioma (m)	foreign (language)
inadecuado/a	inadequate
informática (f)	ICT
inglés (m)	English
injusto/a	unfair
instituto de segunda enseñanza (m)	secondary school
instituto para alumnos de 16 a 18 años (m)	sixth form college
intercambio (m)	exchange
italiano (m)	Italian
justo/a	fair
laboratorio (m)	laboratory
lápiz (m)	pencil
latín (m)	Latin
lengua (f)	language
libro escolar (m)	school book
listo/a	clever
matemáticas (f/pl)	maths
mochila (f)	school bag
música (f)	music
muy buena nota (f)	very good mark
pasillo (m)	corridor
patio de recreo (m)	playground
pegamento (m)	glue
perezoso/a	lazy
pizarra blanca (f)	whiteboard
pluma (f)	fountain pen
polideportivo (m)	sports hall
portero/a (m/f)	caretaker
practicar	to practise
pregunta (f)	question
progreso (m)	progress

proyector (m)	projector
prueba (f)	class test
química (f)	chemistry
regla (f)	ruler
reunion (f)	assembly
rotulador (m)	felt-tip pen
sacapuntas (m)	sharpener
sala de actos (m)	school hall
sala de profesores (f)	staff room
suspender (un examen)	to fail (an exam)
tarea (f)	task
tijeras (f/pl)	scissors
título (m)	qualification
trabajador/a	hardworking
trimestre (m)	term
uniforme (m)	uniform
universidad (f)	university
vacaciones de verano (f/pl)	summer holidays
vestuario (m)	changing room

asignatura obligatoria (f)	core / compulsory subject
asignatura optativa / facultativa (f)	optional subject
auriculares (m/pl)	headphones
ausente	absent
ciencias empresariales (f/pl)	business studies
derecho (m)	law
dotado/a	gifted
ensayo (m)	essay
examen de fin de curso (m)	final exam
hacer novillos	to play truant
internado (m)	boarding school
lector(a) (m/f)	foreign language assistant
pasar lista (f)	to take the register
reunión nocturna para los padres (f)	parents' evening
sociología (f)	sociology
título (m)	degree (university)
traducción (f)	translation

Now try this

What GCSEs are you and your friends taking? Check you can translate them all into Spanish. If you're thinking about doing A levels, can you translate those too?

Answers

Personal information

1. Birthdays
1 2 July

2 2 June

3 1973

2. Physical description
(a) blond

(b) fat

(c) green

8. Hobbies
1 D

2 F

3 E

10. Arranging to go out
1 friend

2 Sunday

3 8.10

12. TV programmes
1 10.00

2 09.00

3 08.00

13. Cinema
Alejandro – thrillers, most exciting
Sonia – cartoons, funny

14. Music
4, 5, 7

15. Online activities
4, 6, 8

17. Breakfast
1 They get good results at school.
2 It should be healthy, balanced and tasty.
3 You should avoid drinking them.

18. Eating at home
1 used to eat meat
2 organic vegetables
3 it's healthy

21. The body
1 when he was running
2 since the day before yesterday
3 rest

Out and about

24. Signs in town
Teresa – Piscina
Marta – Estación de autobuses
Feliciano – Cajero
Alicia – Prohibido fumar
Rico – Prohibido aparcar

25. At the train station
1 in 10 minutes
2 yes
3 It will be late.

26. Weather
1 Bilbao
2 cold
3 hot

27. Places in a town
1 behind the sports centre
2 to the cinema
3 it's nearby

29. Town description
4, 6, 8

32. Staying in a hotel
3, 4, 7

33. Staying on a campsite
1, 4, 5

39. Directions
2 F 3 D 4 A
5 E 6 B

40. Transport
1 underground – quick
2 bus – more environmentally friendly
3 coach – cheaper
4 plane – more comfortable

41. Buying tickets
1 15.40
2 tomorrow
3 79 euros

Customer service and transactions

43. Eating in a cafe
2 María

3 Miguel

4 Ana

45. Opinions about food
1 healthy
2 she doesn't have time
3 really tasty

46. Restaurant problems
A, C, E

48. Shops
1 5

2 3

3 4

4 1

48. Shopping for food
1 the town hall
2 500 euros
3 mushrooms

49. At the market
C, D, H

50. Signs in shops
D, G, H

52. Shopping for clothes
1 Ana
2 Juan
3 Ana
4 María
5 Juan

53. Returning items
C, D, H

54. Online shopping
1 *Two of*: payments / returning goods / fraud
2 It's possible that we'll make most of our purchases online
3 to be as careful online as they are in actual shops

56. Travelling
1 4567
2 cancelled
3 a strike

57. Travel problems
3, 6, 8

58. Money problems
1 taking money from the cashpoint
2 *Two of:* she bumped into a tree, fell on the pavement, twisted her ankle
3 *Two of:* bald, with a moustache, with a tattoo on his left arm
4 silver earrings
5 they were a present from her grandmother

59. Lost property and theft

Item	bracelet
Description (two details)	gold, not expensive
Where exactly	the shop's changing rooms
When	this morning

60. Complaints and problems
Julia B
Martín C
Jaime D
Mr Sánchez E

Future plans, education and work

61. School subjects
1 Francisco 2 Francisco
3 Marcela 4 Francisco

63. School routine
C, D, F

69. Jobs
2 fireman
3 he didn't like working at night
4 waiter
5 plumber
6 you can earn a lot of money

70. Job adverts
1, 4, 6

71. CV
1 (a)

2 (c)

3 (a)

4 (a)

73. Job interview
2, 5, 6

74. Opinions about jobs
1 the responsibility
2 works a lot

76. My work experienc
C, D, F

78. Dialogues and messages
2 667 78 96 78
3 Iberia
4 Monday to Friday, 9am–1pm
5 967 87 81 52

79. Language of the internet
1 don't do it illegally
2 send messages to your aunt in the US
3 the screen and keyboard
4 tell anyone what it is

80. Internet pros and cons
2, 3, 6

Grammar

81. Nouns and articles
1 1 folletos   2 veces
  3 tradiciones 4 cafés
  5 actores
2 1 la   2 el   3 el
  4 la   5 la

82. Adjectives
pequeña, bonitas, ingleses, simpática, habladora, históricos, ruidosos, interesantes

83. Possessives and pronouns
mi, sus, mi, que, su, el mío, él, el suyo

84. Comparisons
1 el peor   2 los mejores
3 la más bonita   4 aburridísimo
5 la mejor   6 el más feo
7 más guapo   8 más perezosa

85. Other adjectives
1 Ese chico es tonto.
2 Esta manzana está rica.
3 Quiero comprar esos vaqueros.
4 Aquella casa es grandísima.
5 Esta película es aburrida.
6 No quiero ese jersey – quiero aquella rebeca.

86. Pronouns
1 Voy a darlo a mi padre / Lo voy a dar a mi padre.
2 La quiero.
3 Voy a comprarlo / Lo voy a comprar.
4 Los vi en Bilbao.
5 Quiero decirle un secreto.

87. The present tense
1 escucho
2 hablan
3 juega
4 quieres
5 comemos
6 encuentran
7 vivís
8 duerme

88. Reflexives and irregulars

1 1 Me   2 se   3 me
    4 nos   5 te   6 se

2 1 conozco – I know / meet
    2 tengo – I have
    3 vamos – we go
    4 pongo – I put
    5 salgo – I go out
    6 traigo – I bring

89. *Ser* and *estar*

1 está   2 es   3 es
4 estoy   5 son   6 es
7 están   8 está

90. The gerund

1 estoy / estaba jugando
2 estoy / estaba escribiendo
3 está / estaba hablando
4 está / estaba durmiendo
5 estoy / estaba comiendo
6 estoy / estaba tomando
7 están / estaban navegando
8 estás / estabas cantando

91. The preterite tense

1 I go to Italy. (present)
2 I arrived at six. (preterite)
3 I surf the internet. (present)
4 He / She listened to music. (preterite)
5 He / She went to a party which was great. (preterite)
6 It was cold and it rained a bit. (preterite)
7 We saw Pablo in the market. (preterite)
8 I played basketball on the beach. (preterite)

92. The imperfect tense

1 trabajaba   2 comí   3 iba
4 había   5 visité   6 lloraba

93. The future tense

1 1 Nunca fumaré.
    2 Ayudaré a los demas.
    3 Cambiaremos el mundo.
    4 Trabajaré en un aeropuerto.
2 1 Voy a salir a las seis.
    2 Voy a ser médico.
    3 Va a ir a España.
    4 Mañana voy a jugar al tenis.

94. The conditional

bebería, haría, practicaría, tomaría, bebería, comería, me acostaría, dormiría, llevaría

95. Perfect and pluperfect

1 He visitado Palma con mi novio. (perfect)
2 Han hecho sus deberes con mi ayuda. (perfect)
3 Habíamos ido al supermercado con Pablo. (pluperfect)
4 Mi hermana ha escrito una carta de amor. (perfect)
5 ¿Has visto mi abrigo? (perfect)
6 Cuando llegó, mis primos habían comido ya. (pluperfect)

96. Giving instructions

1 Write to me.
2 Wait for your sister.
3 Don't tell me.
4 Don't shout!
5 Click here.
6 Don't take photos!
7 Answer the questions.
8 Don't leave everything to the last minute.

97. The present subjunctive

1 When I go to university, I'll study French.
2 I don't think your friend is good looking.
3 When I'm 18, I'll take a gap year.
4 I want you to talk to Pablo.
5 It's not true that English food is horrible.
6 I don't think Italy is the best football team.

98. Negatives

Suggested answers:
1 No como nunca verduras.
2 No tengo ningún libro.
3 No conozco a nadie.
4 Nadie juega a pelota.
5 Nunca hago mis deberes.
6 No me gusta ni navegar por Internet ni descargar música.
7 No tiene nada.
8 No tengo ningún amigo en Londres.

99. Special verbs

1 Me duele
2 Le gusta
3 Me gustaron
4 Les hace falta
5 Le duelen
6 Me encanta
7 Nos quedan
8 A María le gustan

100. *Por* and *para*

1 1 para   2 para   3 por
    4 para   5 para   6 por
    7 por
2 1 para   2 por   3 para
    4 por   5 ✓   6 para
    7 ✓   8 ✓

101. Questions and exclamations

1 d   2 f   3 h   4 e   5 a   6 b
7 c   8 g

102. Connectives and adverbs

1 *Suggested answers*:
    1 Nunca voy a Paris porque es aburrido.
    2 Mientras jugaba al baloncesto, Juan hacía patinaje.
    3 Después de estudiar, iré a la universidad.
    4 Nos gustaría ir a la playa pero está lloviendo.
2 1 tranquilamente (peacefully)
    2 perfectamente (perfectly)
    3 difícilmente (with difficulty)
    4 severamente (strictly)

103. Numbers

(a) las nueve menos veinte
(b) cuatrocientos sesenta y cinco
(c) el doce de junio de dos mil catorce
(d) séptimo
(e) las once y media
(f) setenta y seis
(g) el primero / el uno de enero de mil novecientos noventa y siete
(h) tercero

Your own notes

Your own notes

Published by Pearson Education Limited, Edinburgh Gate, Harlow, Essex, CM20 2JE.

www.pearsonschoolsandfecolleges.co.uk

Copies of official specifications for all Edexcel qualifications may be found on the Edexcel website: www.edexcel.com

Text © Pearson Education Limited 2013
Audio recorded at Tom Dick + Debbie Productions © Pearson Education Limited
MFL Series Editor: Julie Green
Edited by Rosemary Morlin and Sue Chapple
Typeset by Kamae Design, Oxford
Original illustrations © Pearson Education Limited 2013
Illustrated by KJA Artists
Cover illustration by Miriam Sturdee

The rights of Ian Kendrick and Tracy Traynor to be identified as authors of this work have been asserted by them in accordance with the Copyright, Designs and Patents Act 1988.

First published 2013

16 15 14
10 9 8 7 6 5 4 3

British Library Cataloguing in Publication Data
A catalogue record for this book is available from the British Library

ISBN 978 1 446 90353 7

Printed and bound in Slovakia by Neografia

Acknowledgements
The publisher would like to thank the following for their kind permission to reproduce their photographs:

(Key: b-bottom; c-centre; l-left; r-right; t-top)

Alamy Images: Nick Hanna 31, Photos12 13, Picture Partners 66, Pixoi Ltd 74l; **Corbis:** Design Pics 89 (Alicia), Doable / amanaimages 75; **Digital Vision:** 54; **Getty Images:** Iconica / Nico Kai 44, Stone+ / Adrian Weinbrecht 38; **Pearson Education :** Footsteps Productions Ltd 69; **Pearson Education Ltd:** Ben Nicholson 43, Clark Wiseman / Studio 8 82, 86, Jon Barlow 21, Jules Selmes 47 (Book shop), 57, 100 (Boy), MindStudio 77, 83cl, 83cr, 83br, 84, Sophie Bluy 5, 7, 8, 11, 22, 62, 64, 74r, 85; **Shutterstock.com:** a9photo 42 (Chorizo), Adisa 47 (Cake shop), barbaradudzinska 42 (Ham), CGissemann 42 (Gazpacho), Darren Blake 93, debr22pics 100 (Presents), Giles Romero 42 (Spanish Omelette), I. Quintanilla 58, Joshua Haviv 91, Liza1979 47 (Clothes shop), Michael Cattle 56, Moises Frenandez Acosta 42 (Prawns), Monkey Business Images 78, nito 42 (Meatballs), Nitr 18, Phil Jones 42 (Olives), PhotoBarmley 28, Przemyslaw Ceynowa 53 (Shoes), RamonaS 89 (Roberto), Rob Marmion 6, Sergio Martinez 42 (Paella), Stephen McSweeny 53 (Boots), Willee Cole 71; **Veer/Corbis:** alexraths 73

All other images © Pearson Education Limited

Every effort has been made to contact copyright holders of material reproduced in this book. Any omissions will be rectified in subsequent printings if notice is given to the publishers.

In the writing of this book, no Edexcel examiners authored sections relevant to examination papers for which they have responsibility.